Listen to Your Child

A Practical Guide to Understanding ADHD, Simplifying Family Life with Effective Parenting Strategies &Unlocking Your Child's Potential

Chloe J. Boulding

Table of Contents

Copyright

Introduction

ADHD is a neurodevelopmental disorder that impairs children's ability to concentrate, control their impulses, and focus on tasks. Many children with ADHD struggle to learn and interact with their peers, which can lead to a variety of problems in the classroom and at home. This book is intended for parents of children with atten- tion-deficit/hyperactivity disorder (ADHD), whether or not their children are currently receiving treatment. It will help you under- stand ADHD better and steer you and your child in a different direc- tion. You will learn new strategies for preventing ADHD behavior and assisting your child in meeting expectations more effectively on his own and through communication with others. You'll realize that ADHD isn't a chronic condition. ADHD is something your child does, not something he has. It is a personality trait rather than a medical condition.

Fortunately, there are methods for assisting children with ADHD in better managing their emotions, focusing, and interacting with others. If you have a child with ADHD, you should learn about the disorder, its possible causes, and how you can help your child cope with its symptoms. ADHD can cause a variety of problems in children and adolescents, but there are several things you can do to help. You must control your reaction to your child with ADHD. You will only harm your child and yourself if you give in to your frustration.

To successfully parent a child with ADHD, you must employ a variety of techniques. Traditional methods will frequently leave you disap- pointed and frustrated; alternative methods will make parenting easier.

Parenting a child with ADHD is difficult, but when managed proper- ly, ADHD makes children more creative, resilient, and able to think outside the box. This book will teach you how to manage your child's

ADHD so that what can be a crippling disorder becomes a source of superpowers.

As a result, you will have a new perspective on ADHD, and your relationship with your child will change.

You'll learn new strategies for preventing ADHD behavior and how to help your child meet expectations on his own and in social situations. ADHD is not a chronic medical condition, as you will discover. ADHD is something that your child has rather than a disorder. It's a pattern of behavior, not a disease.

Raising a child with ADHD can be stressful and overwhelming, but there are many things you can do as a parent to help manage symptoms, get through the day, and calm your family down.

Despite everything, I hope you find hope in this book. I hope your family has a variety of options. I hope this isn't the best it'll ever be. I wish you, your family, and your ADHD son the best of luck in the future. This book contains effective natural therapies for treating your child's ADHD symptoms. Let's get started.

Chapter 1: What Is ADHD and How Is It Diagnosed?

What Is ADHD?

ADHD is a neurodevelopmental disorder characterized by difficulty paying attention, impulsivity, and hyperactivity. These symptoms frequently cause problems in a person's daily life, such as at school or work, social functioning, and interpersonal relationships.

Although ADHD is most commonly diagnosed in children, it can also affect adults. A combination of genetic, environmental, and neurological factors is thought to be responsible. ADHD symptoms often improve with age, but many people continue to struggle with attention and impulsivity throughout their lives. It is a common childhood disorder that can persist into adulthood. A combination of medication and therapy is usually used to treat it.

While attention deficit hyperactivity disorder (ADHD) affects children and teenagers, it is more prevalent in adults. ADHD is the most commonly recognized mental health condition in children, and boys are more likely to be affected than girls. Children with ADHD frequently have difficulty focusing or paying attention. They don't appear to be able to follow instructions and are frequently bored or angry. Furthermore, they are impulsive and move constantly without pausing to think.

ADHD is typically treated with a combination of medications like stimulants and behavioral therapies like cognitive-behavioral therapy. The goal of treatment is to assist someone with ADHD in managing their symptoms and leading a fulfilling and successful life.

It is critical to understand that ADHD is not a single disorder, but rather a collection of symptoms caused by a variety of underlying issues. It's also worth noting that ADHD can be managed and treated. Children with ADHD can lead successful lives with the right support.

It's important to note that the severity of ADHD symptoms can vary greatly between people. Some people with ADHD may have mild symptoms that can be managed with self-regulation strategies and accommodations, whereas others may have severe symptoms that interfere with daily functioning.

People with ADHD struggle to control what their behaviors do or say. They may be impulsive or act without thinking first, and they may act without regard for the consequences to themselves or others, disrupting the lives of others. These people typically struggle to pay attention to details such as the dates on documents or the names of their classmates; they make careless mistakes when completing schoolwork; and they may struggle with organization and time management. Some people are easily distracted by what others say.

ADHD can also have an impact on academic performance in school because children with ADHD may struggle to focus on work, follow directions, and make decisions. They may also be forgetful or misplace items such as books, pencils, or toys. As a result, children and adults with ADHD may get into a lot of trouble due to disruptive behavior because they miss important information from the teacher or do not complete their homework on time due to the constant distrac- tion they face in class or online at school. Because there is such a large gap between their best efforts and the outcome of the work, these people may struggle with their self-esteem because they believe they will never be able to keep up with other people.

ADHD is treatable, and many people can significantly improve their symptoms with medication and positive behavioral support for those who live in households with ADHD.

According to the NIMH, approximately 1-3% of preschool children are diagnosed with ADHD, while the rate rises to 5-10% among elementary school children and up to 20-30% among high school students. It is estimated that approximately one-quarter of all ADHD children will continue to have symptoms as adults. ADHD affects four times as many boys as girls.

ADHD affects people all over the world, and there is evidence that the disorder is becoming more common in both children and adults. This has been attributed to many factors, including increased rates of diagnosis, increased attention to the disorder by medical professionals, changing diagnostic criteria, improved detection using modern technology such as brain imaging, and medication treatment becoming more widely available.

Children with ADHD may struggle to interact with their peers because they are easily distracted and have difficulty paying attention.

ADHD can significantly impact a child's life, as it can cause them to struggle in school, have difficulty making friends, and become frustrated or overwhelmed. Children with ADHD must receive the support and resources they need to manage their symptoms and reach their full potential.

Positive Sides of ADHD in Kids

It's clear that having a child with ADHD can be challenging. From the never-ending stream of energy to the constant messes and missed homework, it can be easy to get caught up and simply focus on the negatives. But it's important to remember that there's a positive side to ADHD, too. In fact, many of the qualities that are considered "symptoms" of ADHD can actually be strengths in disguise.

Creativity and Inventiveness

One of the most common positive aspects of ADHD is creativity. Kids with ADHD often have very active imaginations, and they're usually attuned to things that other people might miss. This can lead to all sorts of inventive solutions to problems, both big and small.

For example, a child with ADHD might come up with a new way to organize his room that nobody else has thought of before. Or he might think of a creative solution to a problem at school. Either way, harnessing this creativity can be a huge asset.

Spontaneity and Energy

Another common "symptom" of ADHD is spontaneous behavior and excess energy. While this can be very frustrating at times, it can also lead to some really fun moments. Kids with ADHD are often the life of the party, always ready with a joke or a funny story. And their energy can be infectious, helping to bring others out of their shell.

Being Hyper Focused

Finally, many kids with ADHD have what's known as "hyperfocus." This means that they can become so engrossed in an activity that everything else falls away. While this might not seem like a positive trait at first glance, it can actually be quite useful. When directed in the right way, hyperfocus can lead to greater success in school and in extracurricular activities like sports or music. It can also help kids develop greater expertise in their areas of interest.

Types of ADHD

ADHD is classified into three subtypes: inattentive, hyperactive-impulsive, and combined.

People with this subtype of ADHD have difficulty paying attention and are disorganized and forgetful. They may struggle to follow instructions, complete tasks, and maintain sustained focus on a single activity. They may also be prone to careless mistakes and struggle to stay on topic during conversations.

People with hyperactive-impulsive ADHD have difficulty controlling their impulses and may act on them without considering the consequences. They may interrupt others, act rashly, and struggle to wait their turn. They may also be restless and have difficulty sitting still.

Combined type is the most common subtype of ADHD and involves symptoms of both inattention and hyperactivity/impulsivity.

ADHD-Related Symptoms in Children

Attention Deficit Hyperactivity Disorder (ADHD) is a chronic condition that affects millions of children worldwide. Symptoms associated with ADHD in children include:

- Difficulty paying attention, difficulty sustaining focus, easily becoming distracted, impulsivity, hyperactivity, restlessness, and fidgeting

- Often daydream

- Often lose or forget stuff

- Wriggle or fidget

- Talk excessively

- Take needless risks or reckless actions

- Have trouble avoiding the temptation

- Have trouble getting along with friends

- Difficulty taking turns

Raising a child with ADHD is different from regular childrearing. Depending on the nature and severity of your child's symptoms, normal rule-making, and home routines may become nearly impossible to maintain, necessitating a variety of approaches. Even if dealing with some of your child's ADHD-related behaviors is unpleasant, there are ways to make life easier.

Their parents must recognize the functional differences between the brains of ADHD children and other children. Even if they understand what is appropriate and what is not, children with ADHD are more likely to engage in impulsive behavior.

ADHD Diagnosis

Do your children frequently forget things, become easily distracted, or lack organization? If this is the case, ADHD could be to blame. When you see your noisy, restless child, do you suspect ADHD? It's important to remember that diagnosing ADHD is more difficult than it appears. None of the ADD symptoms are abnormal on their own. Most people experience moments of disorganization, distraction, or restlessness. Even persistent hyperactivity or impulsivity does not imply ADHD.

ADHD, formerly known as ADD, cannot be diagnosed with a single physical or medical test, or other tests. To determine whether you or your child has ADHD, you or your child will need to see a specialist or other healthcare professional. To rule out other potential sources of symptoms, you may plan to use a variety of techniques, such as a list of symptoms, responses to inquiries about previous and current issues, or a physical exam.

Remember that symptoms of ADHD, such as inability to focus and hyperactivity, can be confused with other conditions and difficulties, such as emotional issues and learning difficulties, which require entirely different treatments. Getting a thorough evaluation and diagnosis is critical because just because something appears to be ADHD does not mean it is.

Because each child's symptoms are unique, healthcare practitioners may use a variety of criteria to diagnose ADHD. It is critical, to be honest, and open with the professional conducting the assessment to ensure the most effective outcome possible.

To be diagnosed with ADHD, your child must exhibit a combination of the three impulsivity, inattention, and hyperactivity symptoms. When evaluating the issue, the mental health expert will also consider the following factors:

- How severe are the symptoms and signs? To be identified, your child must experience negative effects from ADHD symptoms. People with ADHD frequently struggle in one or more areas of their lives, such as their careers, income, or familial obligations.

- When did the first signs appear? Because ADHD typically manifests in childhood, the therapist or counselor will consider how long ago the symptoms first appeared. Can you trace your symptoms back to your childhood if you're an adult?

- How long have the symptoms bothered your child or you? Before ADHD is diagnosed, symptoms should have been present for at least six months.

- When and how do the signs appear? ADHD symptoms, for example, must manifest in the home and in the classroom. If the symptoms appear only in one setting, ADHD is most likely not to blame.

Even if you are certain that your child has ADHD, you cannot diagnose it yourself and then treat them with over-the-counter medication.

You must defer to medical professionals who are trained in this area. They will be able to determine whether your child has ADHD or another disorder. You also want to avoid a misdiagnosis, which could be disastrous. It's important to know the procedure of the diagnosis process. There will be no blood, urine, or brain scans to prove or disprove ADHD. A comprehensive evaluation is performed, followed by treatment by primary care doctors and specialists such as pediatricians, psychiatrists, psychologists, and neurologists, especially when other factors such as the previously mentioned coexisting learning problems and mood disorders affect the diagnosis.

So after liaising with the school you would next consult with the doctor. Have your notes and questions ready. Remember to have the school's report ready too. If the doctor suspects it's ADHD, he will refer you to an expert for the actual evaluation process. Or the counselors at your child's school could help with this. You have to be completely honest with the healthcare professional you talk to. Again, have your notebook with you, and have your questions written down. Ask for a contact number so that if you think of anything else you can contact the expert. That little bit of information might be what they need to make a positive diagnosis. Have this professional diagnosis given to you in writing.

How to Accept Your Child's ADHD Diagnosis

We all hope to bring healthy, happy children into the world who will grow up to have even healthier and happier lives. Unfortunately, genetics as well as a series of other factors sometimes leave their mark on how our children are. An ADHD diagnosis can leave you, as a parent, feeling like you've done something wrong. It could make you feel helpless and hopeless. And, in the end, it could affect you as much as it does your child.

Feeling overwhelmed by sadness, anger, and anxiety once your child has received an ADHD diagnosis is perfectly normal, but it is not something you should dwell on for too long. Taking action as soon as possible and learning how to help your child manage their condition as well as how you should manage your own sensitive situation are both crucial steps you need to take forward.

The very first thing to do is learn more about Attention Deficit Hyperactive Disorder. Since you are here reading this book, it is quite clear that you are already on a good path in this respect and that you want to educate yourself more on this topic.

This is a challenging task, so don't feel like your child is the only one who has to work at accepting his or her ADHD diagnosis and its potential consequences. As you take in what you've learned about ADHD, and as you begin to understand the many facets of the condition in greater detail, you're also learning more about yourself and how well you manage stress. You are learning about your child's needs too.

Finding the right type of treatment and therapy for your child's specific needs might take time, so don't rush through everything. Try out the different options your medical specialist recommends, and always be prepared to make adjustments. There's no given recipe for the treatment and management of this condition, so you need to manage your expectations.

Do talk to other parents of children with ADHD. This will not only help you find new tactics and techniques you can use in raising your child but will also help you feel less alone in this endeavor. The community has a powerful impact on us, so surrounding yourself with people who get what you are going through is essential.

Chapter 2: The Causes of ADHD and Current Theories About Its Development

ADHD in children is a complex condition that can have multiple causes. While the exact cause of ADHD remains unknown, researchers have identified various factors that may contribute to the development of this disorder.

Genetics

Will my children have ADHD as well? This is a question that almost all adults ask, whether they have had ADHD for a long time or were only recently diagnosed. The answer is that it varies.

The majority of ADHD cases are inherited. Despite this clear genetic link, having ADHD does not guarantee that your offspring will have it as well. Over 70% of the causes are thought to be inherited. This is due to the fact that a child's proclivity for developing ADHD is influenced by both genetic and environmental factors.

ADHD genes can be passed down to future generations if they are not activated. According to one study, only one-third of men with ADHD had children with the disorder.

Suppose a kid inherits ADHD from a parent, the child's ADHD presentation will not be influenced by the parent's presentation of ADHD (inattentive, hyperactive-impulsive, or mixed).

So far, a number of gene candidates have been identified in ADHD families. According to scientists, the manifestation of ADHD symptoms is caused by the interaction of a number of these genes with the environment rather than by one specific gene.

ADHD has no gender distinction. To put it another way, ADHD does not affect only men, and children do not inherit it from their fathers.

Some people believe that because fathers are the only ones who can develop ADHD, a child cannot develop it. That is not the case.

Despite the fact that men are diagnosed with ADHD more often than women, it's vital to realize that anyone can have ADHD.

Illnesses and Injuries

Illnesses such as meningitis and encephalitis can cause learning and attention problems.

ADHD symptoms can be caused by brain damage, such as an early brain injury, trauma, or another impediment to normal brain development in a small number of people.

According to a study published in the journal JAMA Pediatric, children who have previously suffered traumatic brain injuries, even if they were milder, are more likely to develop ADHD for up to ten years after the injury.

Toxins

When a child is exposed to certain environmental pollutants as a young child, their risk of developing ADHD increases.

Lead exposure at any level can cause hyperactivity and disorientation. Lead can be found in a variety of products, including gasoline and paint from homes built before 1978.

Substance Abuse While Pregnant

A parent's health and daily routines during pregnancy may have an impact on the development of ADHD. Unbalanced nutrition, for example, and disorders affecting pregnant women can increase the risk of ADHD.

There is evidence that taking certain medications while pregnant increases the likelihood of having an ADHD-prone child.

Low Birth Weight and Premature Birth

Many studies have found a link between ADHD and premature birth and low birth weight. The risk has been shown to increase with prematurity, with the risk of ADHD increasing as the birth date approaches. Conversely, as birth weight decreases, so does the risk of ADHD. Babies born at eight months of pregnancy, for example, have higher birth weights than those born at seven months of pregnancy, implying that a baby born in the seventh month is at greater risk than a baby born in the eighth gestational month.

Environmental Risks

People frequently associate ADHD with an unhealthy lifestyle. Parents are frequently told that if they feed their children processed foods and unhealthy snacks, and allow their children to watch too much TV or use electronic devices, their child will "get" ADHD. It is important to note that, while sugar and screen time have been shown to be harmful and contribute to the development of behaviors similar to ADHD symptoms, they have not been linked with the clinical definition of ADHD as a diagnosable disorder.

Diet and Chemical Exposure

Although an unhealthy diet has been shown to harm children's health, it is not directly linked to the development of ADHD. Instead, exposure to some food toxins, such as lead, pesticides, and polychlorinated biphenyls (PCBs), is linked to the illness. These substances have been shown to harm children's neural systems and cognitive functioning. PCBs found in mass-produced foods, in particular, had neurobehavioral effects on children similar to those seen in ADHD. The substance primarily influenced cognitive flexibility, response definition, and working memory. Babies exposed to this substance during pregnancy displayed more ADHD-like behaviors in childhood.

Psychological Adversity

According to research, parental depression, particularly that of mothers, increases the risk of ADHD. When a child lives in a disordered household environment, whether due to parental mental or socioeconomic problems, they experience almost unbearable emotional and psychological distress. The same thing happens when the child's primary caregivers, whether parents or close family members are unsupportive, or when the child grows up in extreme poverty.

Chapter 3: The Potential Co-Occurring Conditions That May Be Associated with ADHD

Around 80% of people with ADHD have at least one other mental illness recognized in them at some time in their life. The most frequent co-morbidities of ADHD are learning disabilities, anxiety, depression, sensory processing disorder, and oppositional defiant disorder.

Autism Spectrum Disorder

Autism spectrum disorder is a neurological condition that affects how a person perceives and interacts with others, resulting in communication and social interaction difficulties. Another feature of the condition is its restricted and recurring behavioral patterns. The term "spectrum" refers to the wide range of symptoms and severity associated with an autism spectrum disorder.

Autism spectrum disorder combines illnesses that were previous- ly thought to be distinct diagnoses, such as autism, Asperger's syndrome, childhood disintegrative disorder, and an unexplained type of pervasive developmental disorder. Despite being considered to be at the moderate end of the autism spectrum disorder, the term "Asperger's syndrome" is occasionally used.

Early autism spectrum disorders cause problems with social, intellectual, and vocational functioning in society. Symptoms of autism in young children are common during the first year. A small percentage of children appear to develop normally during the first year, but when they begin to exhibit symptoms of autism between the ages of 18 and 24 months, they go through a period of regression.

Although there is no known cure for autism spectrum disorder, intensive early intervention may significantly improve the lives of many children.

Bipolar Disorder

Among other symptoms, bipolar disorder in children is characterized by extreme irritability and mood swings. Although there is no known cure for bipolar disorder, children can live normal lives with the help of medication and counseling.

Manic-depressive disease, also known as bipolar disorder or manic depression, is a chronic mood illness and mental health condition that causes abrupt changes in mood, energy levels, thinking processes, and behavior. These shifts can last a few minutes or several days, weeks, or even months, and they make it difficult to perform your daily tasks.

Despite the fact that symptoms can appear in childhood, bipolar disorder is often discovered in adolescence or adulthood.

There are numerous types of bipolar disorder, but the majority of them include manic and depressive episodes. Bipolar people, on the other hand, may not always experience manic or depressive episodes. Another sense that people have is euthymia, which is a fairly continuous emotional state in which they are their normal selves.

During a manic episode, your mood, emotions, energy level, and level of activity are significantly altered and overly heightened. Hypomania, a milder form of mania, may occur in certain bipolar disorder subtypes.

In addition to many other depression symptoms, you may experience low mood, sadness, and/or loss of interest in most activities during a depressive episode.

Children and adolescents are affected differently than adults by bipolar disorder. Adults with bipolar disorder frequently have distinct manic or depressive episodes that last a week or more. Children and teenagers may have fewer clearly defined phases and faster transitions between episodes. A child, for example, may experience bursts of joy and silliness, violent outbursts, and uncontrollable sobs on the same day.

Depression

A child who is depressed may not necessarily experience severe depression. However, if the depression persists or interferes with daily obligations such as work, family, or friends, it may be a sign of a depressive illness. Remember that, despite being a serious illness, depression is treatable.

Childhood depression manifests itself in a variety of ways. Because symptoms are mistakenly classified as common emotional and psychological changes, the condition frequently goes undetected and untreated. Early medical research focused on "masked" depression, in which a child's depressed mood was manifested through acting out or unreasonable behavior. While this may occur, especially in younger children, many children, like depressed adults, exhibit melancholy or depression symptoms. Depression is characterized by sadness, a sense of powerlessness, and mood swings.

Not all children exhibit all of these symptoms. In reality, most people exhibit various symptoms at different times and in different settings. While some children with severe depression may be able to function relatively well in structured environments, the majority of them may notice a change in their social life, lose interest in school, perform poorly in class, or change their appearance. A child may begin using drugs or alcohol if they are over the age of 12.

Anxiety

We've all experienced anxiety at some point in our lives. Anxiety manifests as stress, worry, tension, tiredness, and a variety of other symptoms. The average person's fleeting pressure, on the other hand, is not considered a disorder. Chronic anxiety affects approximately 30% of ADHD children and 50% of ADHD adults. These feelings of anxiety and stress can have a negative impact on the nature of life. The presence or absence of anxiety with ADHD treatment determines whether it is a secondary or comorbid condition.

Disabilities in Learning and Language

A type of learning disorder affects up to 50% of ADHD children. This figure is quite compelling when compared to only 5% of non-ADHD children having learning disorders. Two of the most common learning disorders that can affect an ADHD child are dyslexia and dyscalculia. Dyslexia affects a child's ability to read and write. Dyscalculia impairs a child's ability to comprehend and execute math skills. Language disorders affect about 12% of ADHD children, but only about 3% of non-ADHD children have these speech problems. Learning and language disabilities are both considered comorbid conditions. They each require their treatment strategy.

Difficulties with Gross and Fine Motor Skills

Fine motor skills include tasks such as writing and grasping a pen- cil with your fingers. Physical activities such as jumping and running are examples of gross motor skills. Both types of gifts necessitate the use of specific small or large muscle groups. ADHD can impair your child's fine and gross motor skills. You may notice, for example, that your child struggles to write neatly because their hand and fingers jerk around. Because ADHD affects larger muscle groups, your child may appear awkward and clumsy, such as falling frequently or struggling to do a jumping jack. These are comorbid conditions that necessitate their treatment plan.

Obsessive-Compulsive Disorder

OCD, or obsessive-compulsive disorder, may conjure up images of television hoarding shows. While hoarding is a symptom of OCD, it is not the only one. This condition can be mild or severe. It can appear as repetitive behavior, such as counting to a certain number while performing a task or even pulling out hair. OCD can also include an extreme need to be clean, such as repeatedly washing hands until they are raw. OCD can manifest as hoarding, which is an overwhelming desire to collect specific items, or as extreme anxiety to the point of being overly cautious. OCD is a comorbid condition as well. Treatment, as well as possible medications, can be beneficial.

Oppositional Defiant Disorder (ODD)

Oppositional defiant disorder (ODD) is a common condition associated with ADHD. This disorder causes extreme bouts of rage and anger. That is not your typical tantrum. ODD is an uncontrollable outburst of rage that occurs during a meltdown caused by even the smallest trigger. These meltdowns can last a few minutes or up to half an hour. When an ODD child has a breakdown, he or she is usually quite remorseful about what happened after calming down. This condition can be secondary or comorbid. There are various treatment options available.

Conduct Disorder

Conduct disorder is a pattern of conduct in children who repeatedly violate others' rights or basic social standards. The child often displays these behavior patterns in several contexts, including at home, school, and in social interactions, and they cause considerable impairment in social, academic, and familial functioning. A high level of uncontrollable aggressiveness characterizes this condition. Children with CD are more prone to injure themselves and others severely. They have a propensity for breaking regulations and causing intentional harm to others' belongings.

Around 25% of children with ADHD have been identified with at least one behavioral or conduct disorder. Early treatment, as usual, may make a huge difference.

Disruptive Mood Dysregulation Disorder

Throwing fit is a normal part of growing up. Many parents have the ability to foresee the circumstances that can "kick off" an emotional episode in their kids. You could think about getting your kid tested for disruptive mood dysregulation disorder if they are throwing tantrums that are out of proportion, difficult to regulate or appear to occur all the time (DMDD).

It is most commonly diagnosed in children. The most noticeable symptoms are irritability, emotional dysregulation, and behavioral outbursts. Outbursts are typically manifested as violent temper tantrums.

DMDD is considered a depressive disorder. A clinically significant decline in mood is a distinguishing feature of all depressive diseases. A person's internal emotional state is referred to as their mood.

Others may interpret DMDD-related mood swings as rage and impatience. The primary symptoms of DMDD that distinguish it from other mental illnesses are as follows:

- Extreme rage tantrums can manifest as either verbal or behavioral outbursts (yelling, screaming) (physical aggression toward people or things).

- Unusual rage outbursts for a child of that age: Tantrums are common in toddlers, and older children yell frequently when they don't get their way. Tantrums in DMDD are not as frequent or as forceful as you might expect given the child's developmental stage.

- Tantrums can occur anywhere, so DMDD may not be the correct diagnosis, for example, if a child only exhibits tantrum behavior when they are with a specific parent or caregiver. A diagnosis requires the presence of symptoms in at least two distinct settings, such as at home, school, or among peers.

When a child has ADHD and a co-occurring disorder, a healthcare provider may choose to treat the ADHD first because treating ADHD first can reduce stress, increase attentional resources, and improve the child's ability to manage the symptoms of the other condition. ADHD treatment options include medication, behavior therapy, skill training, counseling, and educational support and adjustments. These treatments can be tailored to the needs of the children and their families. They can help the patient control their symptoms, cope with their condition, improve their overall psychological well-being, and manage social interactions.

Chapter 4: Biggest Frustrations of Parents of Children with ADHD

Difficulties in School

Moms of ADHD children understand how difficult school can be on a daily basis. It's difficult enough to stay on top of homework, projects, and tests when you're focused and organized. When you have ADHD, however, these things can seem impossible.

One of the most common and visible difficulties that children with ADHD face is difficulty in school. ADHD can make it difficult for children to pay attention and stay focused, making it difficult for them to keep up with their classmates. This can result in frustration and a sense of being overwhelmed.

Let's take a closer look at the three most common school problems that kids with ADHD face.

Executive Function Impairment

This is the ability to plan ahead of time, organize thoughts and materials, and stay on track. Because executive function skills are frequently lacking in ADHD children, they may struggle to complete long-term projects or keep track of multiple tasks at once. It can be difficult to complete assignments on time or remember to turn in homework if you lack strong executive function skills.

Disruptive and Inattentive Behaviors

Many children with ADHD struggle to stay on task and pay attention in class. This can result in disruptive behaviors such as speaking out of turn or frequently getting up from their seat. Children with ADHD may struggle to sit still, follow directions, or wait their turn. These behaviors can irritate both children and adults.

Problems with Learning and Retention

Another challenge faced by kids with ADHD is difficulty retaining information. This can make it hard to learn new material or remember what was learned in the past. Things like forgetfulness, distraction, and disorganization can all get in the way of understanding new material or remembering what was taught in class. This can make schoolwork feel twice as hard as it already is.

Struggles in Their Personal Relationships

It's not hard to see that kids with ADHD have a hard time in school. But what about their personal relationships? Many kids with ADHD struggle with social behavior, and this can lead to difficulties in making and keeping friends. Additionally, they may be bullied by others. Let's take a closer look at the struggles of ADHD kids in personal relationships.

Difficulties with Social Behavior

One of the most challenging aspects of ADHD is dealing with the social ramifications of the disorder. Many kids with ADHD have trouble reading social cues and often say or do things without thinking about the consequences. This can lead to difficulty in making friends and maintaining relationships.

Isolation and Loneliness

A child with ADHD may avoid or disengage from others, and this can lead to isolation and loneliness. Additionally, they may have trouble reading social cues and responding appropriately. As a result, they may come across as socially awkward or even rude. This can be a major obstacle to making and keeping friends.

Bullying by Others

Additionally, ADHD kids may be bullied by others. This is often due to their social awkwardness or because they are seen as different. Being bullied can further damage their self-esteem and make it even harder for them to make friends.

What Are the Effects on Other Children/Siblings?

Siblings of a child with ADHD require more understanding and patience than their age allows, resulting in more frequent and severe conflicts and fights. Having an ADHD sibling can be challenging for their brothers and sisters as well. Siblings may feel less loved or important in this context. Aside from this, they also might feel a dose of guilt for being healthy. In fact, this guilt can be so intense that siblings may become anxious or fearful that they will "catch" the illness from their ADHD sibling.

While some siblings choose to avoid unnecessary conflict, others may misbehave to attract their parents' attention. This can lead to additional family conflicts, especially if parents are more tolerant of the child with ADHD while being stricter with their other children. In this situation, children may feel as if different standards apply to them, which can lead to feelings of inequity and rebellion. Furthermore, the extra work required with an ADHD child often forces parents to assign more chores to their other children. The siblings may become irritated as a result of having to do extra work in this situation. Finally, the siblings may be embarrassed to be seen with their family, or they may believe they are different from the rest of their peers.

All of this puts siblings at greater health risks. Parents should keep in mind that other children need their attention as well and that they should devote time to all of their children equally. They should also avoid assigning too many chores and talk openly and honestly about family problems.

Effects of ADHD on a Family

By observing you and other family members enjoy life and getting along, your child also learns about the positive behaviors that they can mimic to better fit in and bond with others. That way, they learn how to do more things that make them and those around them happy, which contributes to reducing unwanted behaviors. Simply put, taking care of your entire family and yourself, as opposed to focusing all the attention on the child with ADHD, creates a "win-win" situation for everyone!

One or more children with ADHD usually mean that the entire unit faces unique hurdles, from more strain on family income, to how much time you have for other children, and of course, the amount of misbehavior and arguments that are yours to manage daily.

In these circumstances, parents must treat themselves and their children with patience and kindness, as all members are affected by the illness. Before you're able to provide training and the right guidance for your child, you need to fully understand how ADHD affects them.

Extra Strain on Parents

The child's condition places additional demands on parents, who must exert greater effort in guiding the child through daily activities. With ADHD, daily activities require more attention, guidance, and effort. As a result, parenting consumes even more energy from the parents than usual. While treating ADHD can be an extra monthly expense, the stress of parenting may impair parents' work performance. Parents may fall behind on their work, and the added stress of dealing with negative feedback can have an impact on a parent's physical and mental health.

Furthermore, many parents need to work fewer hours to contribute more at home. In some cases, one of the parents quits their job entirely to stay at home full-time. All of this can have a negative impact on the family's income, further complicating family relationships. If you recall, one of the significant factors of psychological adversity that worsens not only the symptoms of the child with ADHD but also increases the risk of all family members experiencing anxiety or depression is economic strain.

With daily parenting responsibilities consuming so much of their time, parents may neglect their personal and social lives. This could have a negative impact on their other relationships, such as friendships, work contacts, and relationships with extended family. It can also have an impact on their mental health, increasing their chances of developing anxiety or depression. Parents who have an ADHD child may also wonder whether or not to have more children, which may have a negative impact if they feel forced to give up on expanding their family.

Finally, the extra conflict caused by exhaustion, frustration, and nervousness may harm a partner or spousal relationship. Fortunately, these difficulties do not always have to tear a family apart. Parents can learn to manage conflict in ways that strengthen their relationships with the right guidance and training. In fact, the more challenges a family faces together, the greater the chances of their bond strengthening and growing closer. In family therapy, parents can gain a new understanding of their children's unique gifts by learning about each other's strengths and weaknesses. Instead of focusing on the weaknesses, the family can gradually begin to rely more on each other's strengths to maintain unity. The sooner this occurs, the sooner everyone in a family can live a healthy, fulfilling life.

Chapter 5: Strategies for Success

Create a Plan and Follow It

Children with ADHD are more likely to complete tasks successfully when they follow predictable patterns and occur in predictable locations. You must establish and maintain order in your home to ensure that your child knows what to expect and what to do.

Create a routine. It is critical to establish a time and place for everything to help a child with ADHD understand and fulfill expectations. Make mealtime, homework, playtime, and bedtime routines that are simple to follow and predictable. Before you go to bed, have your child lay out his or her clothes for the next day. Also, make sure that everything they need to bring to school is in a designated location and easily accessible.

Encourage Physical Activity and Sleep

ADHD children frequently have a lot of energy. Participating in organized sports and other forms of physical activity can help them focus on specific skills and movements while also releasing energy in a healthy way. Physical activity has numerous advantages: It improves concentration, reduces depression and anxiety, and promotes brain development. The most important thing for children with ADHD is that exercise helps them sleep better, which can help with ADHD symptoms.

Select a sport that matches your child's interests and strengths. Softball, for example, requires a lot of "downtime," which is not ideal for children who struggle with attention. Team sports like basketball and hockey, which require constant movement, are better options. Yoga, for example, can help children with ADHD improve their mental control while also strengthening their bodies.

Getting enough sleep every night is difficult for adults, but it is even more difficult for children with ADHD. Most parents with ADHD children will tell you that one of the most difficult parts of their day is bedtime, and while doctors will tell you that medication should help improve sleep patterns, don't hold your breath. Many ADHD children have difficulty falling asleep and sleeping through the night. This lack of sleep exacerbates their ADHD symptoms. As a parent, you must do everything possible to ensure that your child gets enough rest. The best way to do this is to limit stimulants, such as electronics before bedtime and sugar. Creating a bedtime routine that encourages relax- ation can also assist your child in winding down.

Create Clear Guidelines and Expectations for Children Who Have ADHD

They require specific guidelines that they can follow and comprehend.

Make the family's behavioral expectations clear and simple. By writing the rules down, hang them in a place where your child can easily read them. Children with ADHD respond especially well to structured reward and punishment systems. It's critical to explain what happens when the rules are followed and when they are broken. Finally, stick to your system and follow through on every reward or consequence.

A smile, encouraging comment, or another reward can help your child's attention, concentration, and impulse control. Focus on posi-tive reinforcement for appropriate behavior and task completion while responding as little as possible to inappropriate behavior or poor task performance. Praise your child for small achievements that you might overlook in another child.

Help Your Child Eat Well

ADHD children are known for not eating regularly. These kids might starve themselves for long periods without eat- ing, then eat everything in sight. The child's mental and phys- ical health can suffer greatly as a result of this pattern. Schedule nutritious meals or snacks for your child regularly, no more than three hours apart, to prevent unhealthy eating habits. A child with ADHD requires healthy food regularly for their physical needs.

Teach Your Child How to Make Friends

For children with ADHD, even simple social interactions frequent- ly present difficulties. They might talk too much, interrupt frequent- ly, or come across as aggressive or "too intense." They might also have trouble interpreting social cues. They may stand out from other children their age and become targets of unwelcome teasing due to their relative emotional immaturity. But keep in mind that many chil- dren with ADHD are extremely intelligent and creative, and they will eventually learn how to get along with others and distinguish between friends and foes. Parents and teachers may be irritated by the fact that peers may find personality traits amusing and charming.

Ignore the Negative

You must tune out the negative individuals in your life when you de- cide to surround yourself with the proper people—supportive people. The majority of people don't understand ADHD, and they certainly don't comprehend kids who have it. You are responsible for choosing the people you associate with, and part of success is creating a team that doesn't include anybody who would undermine you or your kid.

Help Your Child but Set Limits

We always want to rescue our children whenever they're in a rush. It can harm their independence. The more you do things for your children, the more they will rely on you and the less they'll do for themselves.

Be supportive, but let your child do specific tasks by himself. For instance, when it comes to homework, encourage him to work on it without your help. If you have to monitor him, then don't hover. Sit near him, and work on your own. It is an excellent time to tackle unfinished reports, update your blog, and the like.

Exercise your Patience

Patience is a quality that all parents need, but it is especially important for parents of children who explode. While it is natural for parents to "solve" their children's problems and "cure" their children's explosions, most children need time to grow.

Reduce Yourself to Their Level

This means you should consider the situation from your child's point of view. Just because you see something one way does not mean your child will see it the same way. For starters, you are much older and have a lot more life experience. When you compare their experience to your own, this, combined with the explosive disorders factor, can make things very difficult to identify with. Stop making comparisons and try to understand where your child is coming from. This will make your child feel seen and valued for who they are.

Create a Healthy Environment

Your child is greatly influenced by the environment you create in your home. You already know this, but it will become clearer as your child grows older. Make sure your entire household is a healthy and stable environment where your child feels safe. If there is any uncertainty or toxicity, you should be aware that your child will be affected. These incidents will affect their behavior, either directly or indirectly, and may trigger their disorder explosions symptoms.

Promote Wait Time

This strategy can help them control their impulses to think before speaking. It teaches children how to give a momentary pause before replying or talking. You can also encourage them when they do their homework by asking interactive questions about their favorite books, favorite characters, why they like a certain color, what their day was like today, and other conversational pieces so it can help your child formulate better responses.

Research More About Explosive Disorders

Parents need to understand their children's behavior to help them fight the battle. That's why there is a variety of support groups for parents who have children with explosive disorders. Aside from that, there's an influx of reliable sources on the Internet to help you figure out your child.

When you know more, you'll find out that you're able to handle the situation better. You can anticipate problems that might lead to potentially harmful behavior.

Be Involved

It is important to be involved in your child's activities. Not only will this help them have a better understanding of the challenges they face as a result of ADHD, but it will also help them become more knowledgeable about what your child needs (and how to provide this) at any given time. Participate in their various school events and classes—this way, you can see how their day unfolds.

Understand How ADHD Affects Your Child

ADHD is often viewed as a diagnosis, but it is much more than that. You may never fully comprehend how your child feels, but reading and researching, as well as connecting with other parents in similar situations, will undoubtedly assist you in better understanding how ADHD affects your child.

Concentrate on Teaching One Thing at a Time to Your Child

One of the most common errors that parents make is attempting to teach everything at once. They believe that their child's ADHD requires them to learn everything all at once, but this will only harm them. This is especially true for more complex subjects such as math and science.

Instead of pushing your child to learn everything at once, try focusing on one thing for a while. The more information you bombard your child with, the more likely their attention will wane, so only "feed" them tidbits of information that are very well-organized and connected.

Try to Be a Good Example

Being a good example for your child is crucial. You must show good qualities and behavior traits, accept your child's mistakes and know how to discipline them in the right way.

Follow what you feel you should do rather than chase after what your child's "presumed" behavior should be. You are their parent, and if you set a good example for them, it should start with knowing that neither your child nor you, are meant to fit into cookie-cutter behaviors.

Spend Special Time Together Every Day

Make time for your ADHD child regularly. Otherwise, they will begin to feel neglected and may act out in response. Discuss their day, inquire about their feelings, congratulate them on their accomplishments, and assist them in finding solutions to their problems. Your child may be young, but they have problems as well. Showing them you're there to help will increase their trust in you while also providing structure and security (which is incredibly important for a child with ADHD).

Break up Tasks

Breaking tasks down into smaller tasks makes things easier for your child, but trying to remember everything they need to do can still be difficult. You can help by making a chart that breaks down all of their tasks. The chart shows them what they have accomplished and what remains to be done.

Organization

Dealing with day-to-day life will be one of your child's daily struggles. Things you take for granted can often overwhelm your child. Many parents believe it is beneficial to organize their homes to provide their children with a respite from the chaos that surrounds them. Find a nice quiet spot in your house where your child can get away from it all. Keeping your home neat can also help because your child will know where things belong. It all boils down to providing structure for your child.

Counseling

Now, this might not be right for everybody, but many parents find it to be truly helpful. Counseling is not going to solve all of your parenting issues, but it is a great resource to turn to. A counselor will help encourage your child in ways that you cannot, but can also provide assistance for you as a parent. They are a great resource to add to your support group. Again, counseling is not something everybody will use, but it shouldn't be discarded without thinking about it first.

Connect with Others for Support and Awareness

Seeking others who are in similar situations can help tremendously. It is one of the most important things you can do for yourself. Be- ing there for others as they go through their challenges, and offering support yourself, will help you maintain a sense of perspective that I could not have otherwise.

Also, joining online forums or maintaining social media pages and groups is a great way to keep up with what's happening in your community and to stay informed about the latest news about ADHD, treatments, therapy, and techniques other parents use with their children.

How Can Teachers Help Kids with ADHD?

Both parents and teachers should see each other as allies when it comes to ensuring the success of a child with ADHD. Some of the things teachers can do to help kids with ADHD include the following:

1   Avoid negative comments and attitudes.

2   Address concerns in private or with the whole class, not one child.

3   Use concrete examples to illustrate points of learning (For example, say "Pick up the math textbook" instead of "Let's do math"). Your child is far more likely to listen if you give them something specific to do to follow along with what you're asking them to do.

4   Listen to the child's concerns and complaints and address them fairly.

5   Use positive reinforcement whenever possible.

6   Keep students' attention during group discussions by making sure everyone is on task.

7   Make rules fair for everyone and make sure they see the point of rules and policies especially when it comes to disciplinary issues.

8   Realize that kids with ADHD are more likely to blurt out or say things they shouldn't have said so don't make a big deal about it.

9   Avoid arguing disputes with students, as this could de-focus a child with ADHD and make them feel confused.

10   Don't become impatient if your student fidgets in class. Remember that they do not want to be this way and that your goal is to help them stay focused.

11   Avoid talking too much, especially in front of the child when you know they can't keep up. This is almost impossible, so don't beat yourself up over this one. Have an action plan and stick to it.

Instructions for Teaching Kids with ADHD

Teaching children with Attention Deficit Hyperactivity Disorder (ADHD) can be both challenging and rewarding. These step-by-step instructions will assist you in teaching and supporting children with

ADHD in the classroom or at home:

- Understand ADHD and how it affects learning. ADHD is a neurodevelopmental disorder affecting about 5% of children and adolescents. It is distinguished by difficulties paying attention, impulsivity, and hyperactivity. Children with ADHD may struggle to sit still, pay attention, and follow instructions, which can have an impact on their learning and academic performance. To effectively support children with ADHD, you must first understand their unique challenges and needs.

- Make your learning environment positive and structured. ADHD children often thrive in a structured, predictable environment. Consider developing a consistent daily routine, establishing clear rules and expectations, and providing visual cues and reminders to assist the child in staying on track. To help the child stay organized and focused, consider using visual schedules and breaking tasks down into smaller steps.

- Give constructive feedback. It is critical to provide positive reinforcement and feedback. Give students an outlet or a template of what is expected of them instead of saying NO, you cannot do this, or NO, you cannot do that. "When you enter class, check the board for your assignments before doing anything else," you can say, or "When you enter class, speak when you have settled in your desk." "Find your seats first, and then you may speak quietly with your friend," you could say. Conversations must cease when I begin teaching."

- Create a classroom structure. The structure is beneficial to all students in the classroom, but it is especially beneficial to students with ADHD. Students are better able to focus because distractions are kept to a minimum. Having row or table captains collect assignments at the end of the day is one of these routines. Make it a point for ADHD students to check in with the teacher, a peer, or the row captain to see if the assignment is understood and if anything needs to be clarified.

- Give ADHD students adequate supervision. Remember that all students require adequate supervision. Ensure that teachers provide your child with the necessary supervision to ensure a safe learning environment.

- Using a variety of teaching methods and learning materials may benefit children with ADHD. Using a combination of visual, auditory, and kinesthetic (movement-based) methods can help keep the child engaged while also improving understanding and retention. You might also think about using technology, such as computer-based learning programs or educational apps, to help the child learn in a more interactive and engaging manner.

- Provide frequent breaks and opportunities for physical activity. Because children with ADHD may struggle to sit still for long periods of time, it is critical to provide frequent breaks and opportunities for physical activity. Consider incorporating movement breaks into your lessons, such as stretching or exercises, or allowing the child to walk around the room. Physical activity can also help with concentration and attention.

- Use positive reinforcement and praise. Children with ADHD

may have low self-esteem and require additional encouragement and support. Recognize and reward the child's efforts and successes by using positive reinforcement and praise. This can aid in the development of confidence and motivation.

- Provide extra help and accommodations. Children with ADHD may require extra help and accommodations to succeed in school or at home. Some common accommodations include allowing the child to stand or move around while working, as well as using visual aids or graphic organizers to help the child understand and retain information.

- Be understanding and patient. Teaching children with ADHD can be difficult, but it is critical to be patient and understanding. Children with ADHD may require additional time and assistance to learn and succeed, but with the right strategies and accommodations, they can make progress and reach their full potential.

- Limit distractions. Children who have ADHD should avoid sitting near doors or windows. Pets should be kept in another room or corner while the student is working.

- Alternate activities necessitate the child remaining seated, while others necessitate movement throughout the room. Physical movement should be incorporated into instruction whenever possible.

- Important information should be written down and kept in an easily accessible location for the child to find and read. Gently nudge the student in the direction of the resource.

- Divide large tasks into smaller tasks and give children frequent breaks.

- Maintain consistent expectations. The rules of the classroom should be unambiguous. Class rules and expectations should be reviewed and amended as needed regularly.

- The homework routine. After school, like the majority of children with ADHD do, allow at least 30 minutes to an hour of free time for playing or watching television.

- Establish a consistent location and time for completing assignments.

- Before beginning the schoolwork, provide the child with a 10-minute warning.

- Children require assistance in reviewing the job and ensuring that they have the necessary materials.

- Allow the youngster to take brief breaks as needed. Getting up and moving around for a few minutes can do wonders for mental clarity and reduce uneasiness. However, maintain vigilance and be prepared to divert the child's focus or answer inquiries.

- Not only should the results be praised, but also the efforts. Perform regularly!

- Verify the task's completion.

- Gather all homework and school resources required for the following day. Everything must be placed in the backpack and stored at the entrance door.

- After schoolwork is complete, enjoy a fun and relaxing activity together.

Chapter 6: How to Handle the Tantrums of the Child with ADHD?

When dealing with your ADHD child's antisocial behavior, it's critical to understand why they act out and throw tantrums, as well as why some strategies may fail.

We must recognize that their bad behavior is caused by ADHD symptoms. They are deserving of our condolences. Imagine growing up with ADHD and being punished for things over which they have no control. Sitting in a chair for long periods or performing a tedious task—the ADHD symptoms of hyperactivity and impulsivity make their reactions to these situations appear malicious, rude, defiant, and violent. They are not, however, doing this on purpose.

Your child does not want to sit still in church; instead, they want to explore the aisles or go outside to play. This isn't because they're trying to be disrespectful; it's just that they don't like sitting quietly for long periods.

Is your child being sent home from school or receiving disciplinary action from teachers and principals because they are not paying attention in class, interrupting, or getting up? Again, they are not active- ly attempting to be malicious toward the teacher or their classmates; their ADHD simply makes many of the tasks required and expected at school extremely difficult.

So, Why Do ADHD Kids Act Out and Have Tantrums?

The answer is simple in its most basic form, but it stems from a complicated history of being disciplined for things over which they have little control.

Imagine being chastised for things you can't help but do. Unfortunately, many children believe that because they are scolded and told they are "bad" for actions they cannot control, they are inherently wicked or bad. This internalized belief can result in aggression toward correction, redirected or taught outbursts, and rebellious behavior.

Homework, chores, and getting ready for bed are all repetitive and boring for children with ADHD. And their ADHD symptoms will do anything to avoid mundane and repetitive tasks. Unfortunately for us, these situations can quickly escalate into war zones because defiance frequently manifests itself in tantrums, screaming, arguing, and power struggles. Children, whether consciously or subconsciously, understand that by throwing a temper tantrum, they will either be excused from doing something or the task will be changed to something more enjoyable. Or perhaps they will only be required to do the bare minimum. The child will then repeat the behavior if the tantrum is successful and they get what they want by acting out in this manner.

Parenting an ADHD child is not the same as parenting a non-ADHD child. This means that disciplinary reactions, strategies, and actions to try to correct poor behavior in your ADHD child may not work. Losing your temper is one technique that will not work on your child. When a child misbehaves on a rare occasion, seeing their parents lose their temper can be enough to set them straight, teach them a les- son, and prevent them from misbehaving in the future. A child with ADHD, on the other hand, will become accustomed to their parents yelling at them. This becomes their new normal, and they begin to believe that they will be yelled at no matter what they do. So why would they stop?

How to Handle Temper Tantrums

Children express their frustrations with various challenges through tantrums. Maybe your toddler is having difficulties completing a specific task. Perhaps they don't have the right words to express what they feel. Frustrations play a major role in triggering anger that leads to tantrums. Let's look at various ways to handle tantrums in children.

The Three Baskets

Dr. Ross Greene, a clinical psychologist and New York Times best-selling author with over thirty years of experience, developed this method of conflict resolution.

It will be exhausting to deal with the frequent meltdowns, tantrums, and outbursts, but learning to separate these conflicts in your mind can make all the difference. This strategy aims not only to help you deal with a disruptive child but also to reduce the number of tantrums and fights and to help your child move away from the belief that this is how they will get what they want in life.

So, What Exactly Is the Basket Strategy?

Dr. Greene's "three basket method" or "basket approach" suggests that parents divide conflicts, disputes, arguments, and points of tension into three separate "baskets." Let us refer to these baskets as A, B, and C.

You can categorize and respond to points of tension and conflict in one of these three categories with your child through patience and practice.

In "basket A," you will record the times when you must command your child's obedience. These are non-negotiable boundaries and necessary safety behaviors. For example, running out into a busy street, buckling their seat belt, hitting or kicking others, and jumping off high things are all examples of inappropriate behavior. These are all important boundaries that you and your child must adhere to.

In "basket B," you will place the moments and tension points where you are willing to allow for some negotiation and to consider alternative solutions and options. These are high-priority behaviors that are important but not worth a massive power struggle or an explosive tantrum. This is possibly the most important basket because it is during the conflict that compromise and negotiation skills can be learned and taught. Consider a "you get some of what you want, and I get some of what I want" approach and do your best to understand your child's perspective while explaining your own.

You will have moments in "basket C" when you don't care about the outcome. These conflicts may have seemed important at the time, but they are not worth the fight or the meltdowns that ensue. These can include disagreements between you and your child about what they wear, what they will or will not eat, and keeping their room clean. There are far better issues to practice negotiating on.

Yelling Isn't the Answer

We touched on this point a little earlier, but this strategy discusses why you should try to refrain from shouting.

Yelling doesn't help the child with ADHD learn better behavior. In fact, this harsh method of punishment can make them act out even more.

We know that children emulate their parents, so it is important to set a good example for them. Young children pay attention to every little thing that goes on around them; this is because they learn through observing. Your home is your child's first classroom, and your child will copy everything you say and do.

Modeling good behavior, not yelling, and practicing patience are not only beneficial for you as a parent but will help your child develop good habits as well.

- Encourage your child to develop patience. Instead of yelling, show your child healthy ways to calm down. For example, pause, take a deep breath, or distance yourself from a situation.

- Stick with a game plan. When you come up with a new technique, disciplinary action, or punishment, your child will fight back even harder. This will make you think the methods and strategies are not working. Children tend to argue back to try and get out of a new and uncomfortable way of living. But you cannot give up when they begin to fight back. You need to stick with your game plan and keep going because once your child realizes they can't throw a tantrum to get out of doing something, they will begin to argue less and less.

- Stay cool. Children with ADHD are often very sensitive to anger. When you yell, they are probably not even hearing what you are saying. They can just hear that you are angry with them. This will then lead to an outburst and meltdown. It can be hard at times, but you must remember to keep your cool in these situations because yelling will only make the situation worse.

- When parenting children with ADHD, you must be consistent in your methods and clear in your expectations. They need to know precisely what they can expect from you. This is because they need to know what will happen if they defy you, and this alone will keep just a little bit more peace between you. This will not be easy, and many parents struggle with staying consistent, but it is vital.

- Interrupt, but don't ignore. You stop bad behavior in its tracks by interrupting harmful activities, tantrums, or fights between your children. For example, interrupt harsh words, or take the dinner plate away from your child who walks in the house with dirty hands and ask them to wash before they eat.

- Be brief, don't chatter. When you keep your words to a minimum and tell your child exactly what you want and mean, there is little to no room for misinterpretation. In other words, when disciplining your child, the fewer words you say, the clearer, more effective, and better understood your words will be.

- Punish fairly, don't overdo it. When you impose a punishment, make sure to take some time to think about whether it is fair or not. The punishment should fit the crime, and if your child sees that you punish unfairly, they will fight back even more.

Raising Your Voice

Sudden loud noises bring silence in virtually any situation, whether it is a board meeting or a toddler tantrum. The instant effect will stop the tantrum, but it is likely to be only for a moment.

A toddler will quickly register your displeasure and react to it by increasing the strength of the tantrum; this is likely even if you continue to rant and rave at them. In fact, the longer you shout at your toddler, the more likely it is that they will simply switch off. Their attention span is generally short, and your rant will have little effect on their tantrum. Of course, shouting can result in your toddler finishing their tantrum.

Ignoring the Tantrum

Is the alternative to shouting simply ignoring your toddler? This approach has more merit than you might at first think. The first step is recognizing that a toddler's temper tantrum occurs because your toddler doesn't know how to control their emotions. Tantrums can be used to help enforce good behavior and help your toddler start to learn how to deal with anger.

Most parents and scientists will agree that the most effective way of dealing with a tantrum is to ignore it. There are two reasons for this:

- Stops the tantrum. Children, particularly toddlers, will respond to how you react. The greater the reaction you offer, the more likely they will be to repeat their actions. However, if they find that their tantrum has no discernable effect on you, they are likely to quickly stop and adopt a different approach. As a toddler, they are testing the boundaries, and your reaction makes a tantrum an acceptable way of getting your attention!

- Little else you can do. In most cases, there is little you can do to stop a tantrum once it has begun, and any form of interaction will be interpreted by your child as acceptance of their tantrum. An attempt to reason with them is likely to fail because you must first get past the tantrum, and even then, they may struggle to understand the reasoning techniques you use.

A temper tantrum is unavoidable, but the following steps will help to ensure that it is dealt with quickly and does not become a regular occurrence:

1 Tell your toddler what they are doing is not going to get them the reward they want; you can even tell them what the consequence of their tantrum will be.

2 Allow them to express themselves. If you are unable to leave them completely, step back and keep an eye on them while ignoring them.

3   If the tantrum occurs in public, it is best to pick up your child and transport them to a more private location, such as your car or a public restroom.

4   If you need to speak to them, do so quietly and calmly. Ignoring them, on the other hand, is the better option.

5   If your child becomes aggressive, you should not ignore them. In this case, it is critical to restrain them to prevent them from injuring themselves or others.

6   Finally, if you know what caused the tantrum, you can take your child out of the situation. You could even try making funny faces or telling a joke to distract them.

7   When your toddler's temper tantrum is over, give them a kiss and a cuddle to reassure them and remind them that the tantrum was unnecessary. Never, ever dwell on the tantrum!

Take the Necessary Precautions to Avoid Tantrums

Make time to play with your child regularly. Allow them to choose the activity and ensure that the child receives your undivided attention. Sharing a positive experience will provide your child with an excellent foundation for calming down whenever they become upset. Examine the opportunities that will recognize their outstanding performance. When a child receives positive reinforcement for a desired performance, they will develop a habit of doing the same.

You can also devise effective strategies for dealing with frustrations immediately, such as taking a deep breath. It's also important to admit when you're upset about something. This is because your child needs to understand that making mistakes is normal. Make sure you understand what caused the tantrum and plan ahead of time. If your child becomes frustrated when they are hungry, try to keep some healthy snacks on hand. If your child begins to complain when he or she is tired, make sleep a priority.

When the Child Yells, Speak Up

Because they want your attention, your toddler will mimic the tone of your voice. Keep in mind that their anger and sadness may help you stay calm. Take the child outside whenever they lose control in a public place, such as a movie theater. Allow them to sit on the bench or in the car while they relax. Having such options will benefit most children, especially if the outburst is caused by a lack of control.

During a post-tantrum, try to fulfill the first demand that triggered the outburst. If the child became agitated because you asked them to collect the toy, they may still be able to obtain it when they are calm. If the child began screaming because you refused to give them a cookie, then give them the cookie once they have stopped crying. Applaud the child when he or she follows through and collects the toy. This is because it is a good habit you will want to instill in them.

Know Why Your Toddler Reacts Strongly

Attempt this one tactic for tantrums for children below two and a half years. In most cases, children within this age bracket have 50 words in their vocabulary and can't link over two words together at a time. The child's communication is limited, but they have countless thoughts, needs, and wishes that must be met. When you fail to understand what they want, they tend to freak out to express their sadness and frustration. The remedy for this is to teach the children how to sign some words like milk, food, and tired. Empathizing with your child is another method to deal with outbursts. It assists in curbing tantrums.

Give Your Child Some Space and Create a Diversion

In most cases, a child is supposed to get rid of the anger. So, just let them do it. This method will help your child know how to vent in a non-destructive manner. They'll have a chance to release their feelings, get themselves together, and recover self-control. This approach can work in tandem with ignoring it a bit.

Offer a Big and Tight Hug

This might feel like the hardest thing to do when your toddler is acting up, but it'll assist them to calm down. This should be a big tight hug and never say anything when doing it. Hugs will make your child feel secure and allow them to understand you care about them, even though you don't support the tantrum habits. In most cases, a child needs a safe place to release one's emotions.

Give Them Food or Suggest Some R&R

The most common causes of tantrums in children are exhaustion and hunger. Because the child is emotionally strained, an outburst will occur quickly. Most parents are perplexed as to why their child has meltdowns at the same times every day—for example, many toddler tantrums occur before lunch and in the evening, which is never a coincidence. If you're experiencing this, make sure your child is getting enough food and water. After that, let her veg, whether that means putting her to bed or watching TV.

Give the Child a Reason to Behave

Some situations can be difficult for children. They can encompass sitting for long hours in a restaurant when eating or staying calm in church. Regardless of the scenario, the tactic is about recognizing when you are asking too much of your child. Also, don't forget to reward them for their hard work.

Laugh About It

You fear public tantrums as a parent for a variety of reasons. You're probably worried that others will label you as a bad parent or that you're raising an out-of-control child. That, however, may entice you to make a decision that will result in deep fits. Even the youngest children are always astute. If you become stressed and angry, let them figure out the best way to end the outburst before many people start staring; they'll figure it out on their own. The best thing to do is suck it up, smile, and pretend everything is fine.

Get Out of That Place

Getting your little one away from the place of a tantrum will subdue the outburst. Additionally, it's an ideal strategy when you're in public places. When your child starts yelling over candy bars or a toy they want, take the child to a different place within the supermarket or even outside until they stop crying. Shifting the place will likely change the behavior.

Don'ts

Don't: Shout

Take a deep breath if your kid got sidetracked and neglected to do her schoolwork. Nothing will change if you shout.

They'll stop listening to you and shut down. It's harmful since your kids are only driven by fear, even if it may seem to "work" in the short term. You want your child's trust. Do not act out what losing control looks like.

Don't: Plan Too Far in Advance

Your kid may not always follow through, even if they don't complete tidying up their dirty room today. Your kids don't need to learn everything right away.

They'll pick up each talent when they're ready with your help and direction. Instead of fretting about what the future could look like, construct it.

Recommended: Learn and practice compassion. The inner workings of your child's brain are invisible to you. You just observe your child's actions. That may be perplexing and frustrating.

Being knowledgeable and sympathetic is helpful, just as it is in any difficult scenario. Read as much as you can about ADHD from reliable sources to better understand the disorder and develop compassion for both yourself and your kid.

Don't: Demand Excessively of Your Child

Children with ADHD struggle to maintain self-control on a par with normal kids their age. They could do well one day and poorly the next. Consistency is too much to expect of kids with ADHD. If you meet your kid where they are at any given time, you'll both feel much better.

Chapter 7: How to Deal with the Parent's Guilt When They Feel Helpless, Frustrated, and Ashamed of the Feeling of Hatred toward Their Child

Does caring for your ADHD-afflicted kid seem like a 24-hour job with little to no downtime? You could have periods of complete exhaustion due to helping them achieve academically, adapting to novel social circumstances, and establishing a regular schedule at home.

However, there are techniques to maintain equilibrium and prevent burnout. Here are a few straightforward suggestions to help you reduce stress while still improving as a parent.

How to Manage Emotions as Parents

It is natural to feel frustrated, hurt, and helpless; however, you must learn how to manage your emotions in a healthy manner.

This can be done by finding support groups and asking for help as soon as you start feeling overwhelmed. If you are frequently depressed or anxious, you should probably seek professional help. There should be NO remorse in that. You, like your child, are going through a lot of changes in your life, so it's perfectly normal to seek assistance.

And, like your child, you may need to examine your behavior and adjust to the new life that awaits you. There IS HOPE for the vast majority of children diagnosed with ADHD—and you must maintain a positive mindset to navigate the bursts of energy, challenges, and potential risks you may face as the parent of a child with ADHD.

Also, just because your child has this condition doesn't mean you have to neglect yourself completely. Take care of yourself just as much as you do your child. After all, if your mental health is deteriorating, you're not helping your child. Exercise, eat healthily, and get some fresh air and sunlight. Similarly, as you begin to learn about the benefits of your child's condition, don't forget to look for your benefits as well.

Take a Break for Yourself

Everyone needs some "me time" to revitalize. Ask your spouse or kid to help out with housework, errands, or other tasks if you feel like you have been working continuously.

Do something enjoyable or calming at least once a week, even if it's only something as straightforward as reading a book, watching your favorite TV program, or having a bath.

Keep Your Relationship Healthy

Try to schedule some alone time each day if you're married or in a committed relationship. Take off your "parent hat," and don't speak about your kids at this time. You might also sometimes have supper together as adults just after you've served the kids their evening meal. Alternately, leave the kids with grandparents, family members, or a babysitter and go on a date without interruptions.

Focus on Your Kid's Cool Qualities

Consider something you love or respect in your kid when their conduct has you gritting your teeth. Each night before you go to bed, consider one of their fantastic attributes. Consider the opposite of that unfavorable trait if you find yourself lingering on something they did that irritated you.

For instance, if they were annoying, you may respect their courage in speaking out. Or maybe the fact that they were also inventive is a silver lining if they drifted off while you were talking.

Control Your Stress

The less stressed you are, the better you will be able to handle the parenting challenges that come your way. Here are a few stress-reduction techniques that work:

When you are frustrated or dissatisfied with your children, don't be too hard on yourself because this happens to everyone at times. Instead, look into your emotions. You might be truthful with a close friend or family member.

Alternatively, you could confide in a therapist or counselor, who can also suggest constructive ways to channel your emotions. It's especially important to seek professional help if you're experiencing fatigue or depression.

Join a Support Group

It may connect you with other parents who are going through similar things. You could share your own experiences and learn from the successes and failures of others. Join a web-based community for parents of ADHD children, or search the internet for local support groups in your area.

Stop Blaming Yourself

ADHD did not develop because you were a "bad parent" to your child. That is not correct. Though experts are unsure of the exact cause, they believe genes may be involved.

Concentrate on things you can change to help your child's symptoms, such as a caring home environment and a regular daily schedule.

Celebrate Their Successes

Take note of the positive outcomes. Even if your child continues to leave the lights on throughout the house, their grades may improve. Change your perspective so that you can see and appreciate what went well. Instead of focusing solely on what you want to change, emphasize the positive.

When your child performs a skill, emphasize the effort and circumstances that led to the behavior. "You finished your assignment," for example. I'm sure you're very proud of yourself. How did it happen so that we can proceed?

Stay Healthy and Think Positive

Parents of ADHD sufferers should set a platform for the children's physical and emotional health. A parent has full control over certain factors that can influence the symptoms of the child's condition.

Positive Attitude Yields Positive Results

You need to demonstrate positivity at all times if you really want to succeed in your endeavor. If you will exude a positive attitude and common sense at all times, then you will be able to bring great help to your child with ADHD. If you are calm and focused, then there is a huge possibility to impart such feelings and attitude to your child and help him stay focused and calm, as well.

Be Honest with Yourself

These are some strategies to make it easier to parent an ADHD child. Depression in adolescents is notoriously difficult to treat. If you are a parent, it is essential that you take care of yourself during this time in your life.

Take a Walk

Working out is a great way to keep your mind and body active and fit. However, you will not always have the time to go to the gym or try an intensive workout routine between catering to your child and your other responsibilities. Thankfully, you can still take a walk. A brisk walk or long stroll can help you clear your head and get some air.

It does not matter what you are doing as you walk; you could use the time to get groceries or take your pets for a walk. The goal is to get some energy from being in a neutral setting.

Meditate

A five-minute meditation routine can help you calm your body and mind while also revitalizing your spirits. If you've never tried meditation before, you can begin by using some guided meditation websites or apps. There are several options available depending on your device and your interests.

Try breathing exercises to help you manage stress while exercising. This way, you can improve your relaxation without having to take a nap. Even though a few deep breaths may not appear to be much, they can effectively calm the body and mind.

If you can manage it, you can involve your child in some of these activities. Meditation, for example, can help them reduce their high energy levels and improve their focus.

Spend Money on Yourself

As a parent, it is easy to become preoccupied with your child and forget that you, too, deserve to be treated properly. Don't forget about yourself. Your earnings should also go toward making you happy. So, take some time for yourself and splurge a little.

Get yourself that jacket you've always wanted. Change or refresh your hairstyle. Take yourself out to dinner. The idea is to do some- thing small for yourself. Take no advantage of the opportunity to over- spend. To avoid exceeding any limits, consider adjusting your budget to make room for saving for this activity. Make an effort to be treated properly because you deserve it.

Play Some Music

Music is another aspect of our culture that influences how we interact with one another and how we feel. It is a soothing form of expression for both the singer and the listener. Music can be therapeutic on its own.

Make time to listen to music or look for new songs that suit your tastes. This is not only a great way to unwind, but it also helps you learn more about yourself.

Furthermore, music can be enjoyed alone or with others. It could be a medium for bonding with your child, such as when you both have a favorite song. So take off your shoes, sink into the couch, crank up the music, clear some space, and set up a dance floor.

Get a Hug

Hugs are therapeutic and can help to relieve stress and tension. But, of course, not everyone is a hugger. However, we cannot deny that hugs feel good, especially when they are genuine, given, and from people we care about, who also care about us.

So, look around you; walk up to your partner, friend, parent, or child, and give them a good old bear hug. They might not get it at first, but they will hug you all the same.

Practice Mindfulness

To be mindful is to be aware of everything going on around you. Unfortunately, between caring for your child and other life responsibilities, everything outside the fire of your mind can easily blur out. This is not great, as it might relegate other essential things to the background. As a result, practicing mindfulness can help you better delegate your attention to your affairs. Also, it allows you to enjoy the moment better instead of questioning what could have been or the future. This way, you can enjoy what is in front of you and give your child a good life.

Make a Smoothie

Smoothies are great and provide the body with tons of nourishment and fuel, thanks to their protein, greens, and fruit content. Having one can be an excellent way to wind down and get back on track before returning to other activities or caring for your child. It is also a healthier alternative to beverages like coffee or soda.

Get Some Alone Time

Some parents' only time alone is when they go to the bathroom. This can be a sobering reality, and you do not want to be in this situation. As a result, it is advised that you take some time to enjoy your own company.

It could take as little as five to ten minutes or as long as several hours, depending on how much time you have available. At this point, avoid doing anything that does not make you feel relaxed. It's time to try that smoothie, do some breathing exercises, and practice mindfulness and meditation. The goal is to recharge before returning to work.

Play Games

Mobile games, video games, and board games are all excellent ways to unwind. Immerse yourself in a game to stimulate your creativity while also enjoying a bit of your competitive edge.

There are numerous ways to enjoy a game, including playing virtually, alone, or against family and friends.

Take the Time to Relax According to Nature Studies, spending time in nature improves our psychological health. A simple hike on a trail, a walk around the park, or even gardening in your yard can help you feel relaxed and rested.

You can also bring nature into your home by using indoor plants. These plants can be difficult to care for, so be certain of your commitment. It may also help you visit the beach and splash around if you live near the coast.

Enjoy Something

There's a lot to do, and time seems to fly by. This rush may cause you to savor things less, so set aside some time in your day to savor something. Make it a habit, from having your first cup of coffee of the day to having breakfast with your family. Keep a Gratitude Journal to help you learn to live in those moments and enjoy them to the fullest.

Focusing on everything that is wrong with you or your child's condition can make it difficult to be thankful. However, gratitude does not come cheap. According to studies, people who keep gratitude journals sleep better and for longer periods of time. Sleep is a valuable resource that you want to enjoy as a parent.

The benefit of keeping a gratitude journal is that you don't have to write in it every day or at specific times; it can be as short as a line of text on any day of the week. Furthermore, it is free and can assist you in refocusing on your rights.

You can make an entry right before bedtime, thanking God for various things. It could be the most basic things or the most complex situations, whatever you want. The general idea is to remind yourself that life is beautiful and that there are things to be grateful for. This could even be added to your child's bedtime routine to encourage them to express their gratitude.

Make a Retreat in Your Bedroom

Clutter in your bedroom can make you less relaxed and more on edge. So it is understandable if you sometimes feel lazy about putting the clothes away after laundry or cleaning and storing shoes properly.

However, caring for yourself also means preparing your living space to facilitate relaxation. As such, your bedroom is an excellent place to start. Turn it into a retreat that makes you want to come back every time. Throw on those comfy sheets and do a bit of decorating. Place that cozy chair near the window, pry apart the curtains, and settle in with a good book and a glass of wine.

With the room decluttered and aired out, you will find yourself nodding off in no time.

Spend Time with Family and Friends

Focusing all your time and effort on your ADHD child could rob you of precious moments with other family members and friends. Finding the balance between self-care, caring for your child, and hanging out with family and friends can be challenging. But you owe it to yourself and them to try.

Including time for me in your schedule is essential. This way, you can plan toward it without compromising other essential things. This is a great self-care tip for balancing your affiliations and avoiding the stress of strained relationships.

Get Enough Sleep

It is essential to keep in mind that proper sleep can give you the appearance of having more time. You may desire to do "just one more thing" or delay going to bed. You'll have greater energy if you get a good night's sleep, which you'll need if you have a child with ADHD to handle daily problems. Determine the amount of sleep you require to feel your best.

The Family Priority Exercise

Try this activity to help your family set their priorities:

- Allow at least one hour for family members to sit down and talk.

- Ask each member of the family to list three things that the family should or should not prioritize. Honesty, support, and health should all be discussed. Explain that this isn't about what you want to do for yourself, but rather what you believe the family should do together.

- Each participant should then "show and tell," revealing his list and explaining why the items on it were chosen.

- Before making any comments, wait until everyone has shared their list. Is there a point on which all family members agree? Is there anything you've forgotten? Do any members of your family appear hesitant to accept your new priorities? Rather than criticizing them, tell them you'd rather hear about what they should be doing rather than their priorities. They will still be able to join in the future.

- Being overwhelmed can have a negative impact on one's health. When you're stressed, you might do or say things you later regret. To avoid this situation, you must prioritize your own needs over the needs of those around you. A parent is more than just someone who loves their child; they, too, have flaws.

ACCEPT ● UNDERSTAND ● LOVE

Chapter 8: The Importance of a Supportive Network, Including the Roles of Family, Teachers, and Healthcare Providers

Working with Teachers and Other Professionals to Support Kids with ADHD

Your kid with ADHD spends a lot of time in school, so it's crucial for them to feel at ease for them to succeed. By working closely with your child's teacher, you can support the development of your child's confidence.

The Value of Collaboration between Teachers and Parents

Collaboration and communication between the family and the school help all pupils have a good education claims LD Online.

Effective parent-teacher communication, teamwork, consistency on objectives and incentives across settings, and joint planning and monitoring of treatments are crucial for kids with ADHD.

The comfort of your kid at school may be greatly impacted by this partnership. Addressing the problems listed below may be greatly helped by your expert understanding of your kid and the teacher's professional expertise.

Your kids with ADHD could have problems staying focused in class and being easily distracted. Find out how to deal with this by speaking with their instructor. It could include locating them on a desk towards the front of the class to reduce distractions.

Discussing different daytime activities with your child to keep them from sitting in their seat all day may also be beneficial. This would entail sitting in a different section of the classroom, perhaps one with plush seats.

If the classroom lacks variety, see if there are any other areas of the school where your children could go for a change of environment.

You can help by talking with your child about their options after their teacher has identified several options. Inform them of what they will be, why you think they will contribute, and what precautions they can take to avoid losing the privilege.

Understand the teacher's position and accept that even their best efforts may not produce the desired results. Fortunately, your participation and collaboration can improve the child's chances of success. First and foremost, be open and honest about the child's condition with the teacher. Don't be afraid to share as much as possible to provide the teacher with a thorough understanding of the child's needs and challenges. Schedule a meeting with the teacher at the start of each school year. They will inform you of the educational objectives, upcoming tasks, and milestones, and you will be able to update them on how your child is doing, what medication they are taking, and how their symptoms have progressed since the last time you saw them.

Create a yearly plan for your child that includes specific educational goals as well as methods and strategies for avoiding symptoms and reinforcing the child's natural gifts and talents. You should speak with the teacher and arrange for a meeting at least once a month, preferably in the classroom. This will allow you to see what their everyday environment looks like. Create general and specific goals with the child and their teachers, such as bringing regular homework, adhering to a study schedule, managing behavior, and so on. Finally, keep in mind that the teacher wants your child to succeed. Pay attention to their advice and opinions, even if they are difficult to hear.

Tips for Activities at Home

As a parent of a kid with ADHD, you are certainly always searching for novel approaches you can take to assist your child in living a better daily life. You could learn something from their instructor that you hadn't before considered.

They may offer advice on how to enhance your child's conduct, as was already indicated. Or, they could be familiar with certain study techniques that your kid might benefit greatly from.

For instance, if you see that your kid struggles to do their homework each night because they can't concentrate long enough to make any progress and have so much to do that they can't afford to take breaks, let their instructor know.

The teacher may be able to provide suggestions, such as reducing distractions at home, or she could work with you to schedule extra study hall periods so your kid can get a head start on their assignments during the school day.

Ask the instructor of your kid everything you can do at home via varied talks. Even while not all of them will be successful, it's still worthwhile to give them a go in order to discover methods to simplify your child's and your own home life.

Discuss Your Combined Strengths and Weaknesses

You may begin to make use of that knowledge if both you and your child's instructor are extremely aware of their talents. For instance, ADHDKidsRock.com lists "an intrinsic sense of curiosity" as one of the traits of children with ADHD among their list of positive traits. To help them enjoy their school days more, find strategies to capitalize on their natural interest.

If you and your kid are both aware of their vulnerabilities, that may also be beneficial. This will ensure that you both understand what has to be done to prevent the problems from recurring throughout the school day. For instance, if interrupting others is a problem for your kid, work with them to make it happen less often at school so they can engage with their peers more effectively.

Guidelines for Working with Teachers

Let's look at some advice that will assist you and the teacher to have the most fruitful connection possible now that you are aware of some of the advantages of working together to make your kid feel more at ease at school.

- Keep in touch regularly. Although the school may schedule parent-teacher conferences on a regular basis, you should probably speak with the teacher more frequently. You will learn any critical knowledge much faster if you do this.

- Discuss the best times and channels for communication. If a teacher is spending extra time working with you, make things as simple as possible for them. You can keep them from feeling overburdened by selecting the most effective channels and times for communication with them.

- Inform your family of any changes that may have an impact on your academic performance. Anything going on at home may have an effect on your child's behavior at school. For example, it may be useful for the teacher to know if your child relies heavily on a schedule that will be disrupted for a few weeks due to a family visit, in case they begin to notice how it affects them at school.

- Don't make situations personal. You may occasionally hear

something from your child's teacher with which you disagree. It can be difficult to hear that your child speaks too much or has difficulty making friends.

- Remember that you and the instructor are on the same team, and they are simply providing you with information to help you.

- Be open to the teacher's advice. If the instructor suggests that your child try a new routine or other test-taking techniques, be prepared to give them a chance. They could lead to significant advancements.

- Together, try out new things. There may be occasions when the instructor or you come upon a technique that is entirely novel to you both. Don't let it prevent you from giving it a go. There is just one way to know if it will or won't work.

Tips to Help Your Family Handle a Child with ADHD

- Remember that your child with ADHD isn't lazy. They are just doing what is easier for them. If they seem hyperactive, it doesn't mean they don't want to sit still. Rather, sitting still is harder for them to do.

- If they seem very impulsive, they are likelier to act before thinking.

- If they struggle at school, remember that this might be because concentrating is more difficult for them than it is for other children, or perhaps the material being presented in class overwhelms them—in which case you should try and see if you can find an alternative educational scenario or a tutor who can come and help out with the academic part of school altogether.

- Make sure your extended family is very well-informed on what ADHD is and how they should behave around your child (and how they can help). Everyone has to be on the same page regarding how the child will be raised and helped from hereon, so be sure that they all understand the importance of adults having the right behavior and using the right techniques with your child.

- You are not alone in this. Support groups, your extended family, and medical providers can all help you navigate the years ahead of you so that you can, in turn, help your child grow healthily and harmoniously.

- Accept that your life will change. Having a child is a significant shift, but knowing that they have ADHD may make you want to be even more disciplined and focused. Your priorities will realign, your house might become a supportive place for raising a child with ADHD, and your perspective on life might change. However, how you handle all of these changes will ultimately determine your success.

- Family members can be a source of support for children and adults with ADHD, even if the person with ADHD doesn't want them to be involved. It's helpful for family members to be aware of their feelings about the disorder because it can help them understand what their loved one is going through. They can also help set up systems that make their life easier, like creating routines and having specific times when they deal with things that might cause problems.

How do others help when they live with someone who has ADHD? What can they do? Here are some tips:

- Be a source of inspiration. If someone with ADHD lacks confidence in their ability to complete tasks, having others in the family remind them of their past accomplishments can help build their self-confidence and set positive goals for the future.

- You may be aware that someone with ADHD has difficulty meeting deadlines or completing projects. Instead of criticizing, show your support by saying things like "I know you can do it," or "You make me so proud." Assist the person with ADHD in setting goals. If a friend with ADHD is having difficulty focusing on his homework, other family members may be able to suggest steps he could take to complete his work, such as reminding him about upcoming weekend plans so that he feels motivated to begin working on it earlier in the week.

- Practice effective communication. When living with someone who has ADHD, family members may struggle to understand why certain tasks are so difficult for them or why they are so forgetful. Communication is essential in any relationship—it's a great way to get along and better understand each other, even if it's challenging at first. Practice discussing problems openly and honestly. Remember that people with ADHD can have difficulty knowing when they've offended you, don't be afraid to speak up if you're upset.

- Remember that people with ADHD are more likely to remember when others are kind or helpful to them. Make an extra effort for your loved one and make sure he knows it. For example, if you know he forgot his lunch, you could stop by on your way to work or school and pick it up.

What should family members refrain from doing? Sometimes peo- ple are so focused on what they can't do that they don't recognize their strengths or recognize problems as opportunities to learn how to change. Instead of focusing on what the person with ADHD does not do, try to identify ways that you can assist rather than criticize the person with ADHD's mistakes. Motivate him or her. Remember that everyone learns at their own pace and in their way. Recognize the person's strengths and express your admiration by saying things like, "I'm so proud of you." It's also critical to learn about ADHD symptom management strategies if you live with someone who has the disorder.

Chapter 9: Importance of Treatment of Sleep and Circadian Rhythm Disorders

Sleep and ADHD

Inadequate sleep exacerbates ADHD symptoms. Stimulants are common ADHD medications that cause an increase in a patient's dopamine levels. This increase in dopamine levels is what helps with ADHD, but it also causes poor sleep.

Patients who are prescribed stimulants tend to sleep poorly or not at all. They may experience daytime sleepiness or lethargy as a result of inadequate sleep. Sleep deprivation can exacerbate ADHD symptoms. It can result in impulsivity, indecision, and inattention. It has also been observed that when stimulants are administered prior to bedtime, patients frequently experience sleep problems.

Sleep is essential to a person's overall health, and a lack of it can lead to difficulties in school and at work due to an inability to understand and concentrate.

A lack of sleep can make anyone less attentive, but children with ADHD may suffer more. Children with ADHD should sleep at least as much as their non-ADHD peers, but they frequently do not. Their difficulty concentrating may result in overstimulation and difficulty sleeping. A regular, early bedtime is the most effective way to deal with this issue, though it may not be enough to completely resolve it.

To encourage your child to get more rest, try one or more of the following methods:

- Reduce your child's television time while increasing their daily activity and exercise levels.

- Caffeine should not be given to your children.

- Establish a buffer period of about an hour before bed to reduce activities. Find gentler activities such as coloring, reading, or silent play.

- Spend ten minutes snuggling with your children. This will give you a sense of love and security while also allowing you to relax.

- Infuse lavender or other scents into your child's room. The aroma may put your children at ease.

- Use background music to relax your child before bedtime. There are various options, including soothing music and natural noises. "White noise" is typically found to be relaxing for kids with ADHD. Put a radio on static or turn on an electric fan to produce white noise.

The Significance of Sleep in the Treatment of ADHD

The symptoms of ADHD may significantly improve with consistent, high-quality sleep. But many children with ADHD have trouble falling asleep at night. When stimulant medicines are the cause of these sleep problems, the issue may be resolved by lowering the dosage or quitting the prescription altogether.

However, a significant portion of kids with ADHD who are not taking stimulants also have trouble sleeping. The advice on the list below might be useful if your kid is one of them.

- Establish a regular bedtime (and enforce it). Try using a sound machine or a fan if ambient noise keeps your kid awake at night.

- At least an hour before going to bed, turn off all devices (TV, computer, video games, iPhone).

- Don't exercise too much in the evening.

- Control sleeping habits. Children with ADHD could have a particularly tough time getting to sleep. Lack of sleep makes recklessness, hyperactivity, and inattentiveness worse.

- It's crucial to support your kids in getting healthier sleep. Stop giving them stimulants like sugar and coffee, and help them sleep better. Create a wholesome, relaxing nighttime routine.

Chapter 10: Tips for Supporting the Emotional Well-Being of Individuals with ADHD and Their Families

Your ADHD child may have difficulty knowing how to express their emotions properly. They may seem overemotional or have outbursts that are disproportionate to the situation. Or they may also struggle with anxiety or depression as a result of their ADHD.

One of the most common challenges faced by children with ADHD is overwhelming emotions. This can manifest as feelings of anger, sadness, or anxiety that seem out of proportion to the situation.

Signs Your Child May Be Struggling to Regulate Their Emotions

There are a few key indicators that your child is having difficulty regulating their emotions. For starters, they may struggle to complete tasks or keep commitments. This can be aggravating for both you and your child, who may feel as if they are constantly reprimanded or told what to do.

Second, you may notice that your child has low self-esteem and is overly critical of themselves. They may also withdraw from previously enjoyed activities or friends. Finally, you may notice that your child is prone to emotional outbursts, such as crying, yelling, or tantrums. These outbursts are frequently triggered by seemingly insignificant events such as not getting their way or being asked to do something the child does not want to do.

Depression and Anxiety

Anxiety and depression are common disorders that co-occur with ADHD. Anxiety disorders affect up to 50% of children with ADHD, and depression affects 30%. This is most likely due to the fact that children with ADHD frequently feel like they are falling behind their peers or are constantly chastised by adults. These conditions can make it even more difficult for children to deal with their intense emotions.

Excessive Emotions

Another common symptom of ADHD is emotional outbursts. Children with ADHD frequently struggle with emotion regulation, which can result in outbursts of rage or frustration. This can be extremely frustrating for both the ADHD child and the adults who care for them.

Children with ADHD may act out to relieve their intense feelings or because they are overwhelmed and don't know how to cope. It is critical to remember that these emotional outbursts are a symptom of ADHD, not a flaw, and that they can be managed with proper treatment.

Other Coexisting Disorders

Children with ADHD are at an increased risk for developing coexisting disorders, such as ODD (oppositional defiant disorder) or conduct disorder. These conditions can make it even more difficult for kids to control their emotions and may lead to disruptive behaviors.

Managing Emotional Dysregulation

Emotional dysregulation is a common symptom of ADHD in children. It refers to difficulty in controlling emotions, which can result in outbursts or meltdowns. Emotional dysregulation can be triggered by events such as changes in routine, having to do tasks that are challenging or frustrating, or feeling overwhelmed.

When a child with ADHD experiences emotional dysregulation, they may have trouble calming down and may act impulsively. Symptoms of emotional dysregulation may include outbursts of anger, tantrums, or crying, as well as mood swings and irritability.

As the parent of a child with ADHD, you know that tantrums and outbursts are part of the territory. But that doesn't make them any less challenging to deal with—especially when they happen in public places.

The good news is that there are things you can do to help your child manage their emotional outburst and avoid meltdowns. With a bit of patience and practice, you can help your child learn to control their emotions and stay calm in challenging situations. Let's take a closer look at some strategies for managing emotions, outbursts, and anger.

Strategies for Managing Outbursts

- Encourage them to express their emotions. This can be accomplished by making time each day to talk about what's going on in their lives. Allowing them to express their feelings, even if they are negative, will make them feel more at ease discussing what is bothering them.

- Make a calming environment in your home. It can be beneficial to create a calm space in your home for your child to go to when they are feeling overwhelmed or angry. This could be a peaceful corner of their bedroom or a spot in the living room where they can unwind with a favorite toy or book. Creating this type of space will provide your child with a safe place to go when they are feeling overwhelmed, as well as help reduce the likelihood of an outburst occurring in the first place.

- Be understanding and patient. It is critical to remember that your child is not deliberately acting out. They are simply struggling to keep their emotions under control. It is critical to be patient and understanding with your child as they learn to control their emotions. Instead of punishing them for having negative emotions, try to understand why they're feeling that way and offer comfort and support.

- Maintain your cool. Losing your cool will only make matters worse. It is critical to respond to your child's outburst calmly and collectedly. Getting angry or yelling will only make the situation worse.

- Take a few deep breaths and count to ten whenever you feel yourself becoming angry. This will help you stay calm and collected so you can deal with the situation more effectively.

- Try to figure out what's causing the outburst and see if you can do anything to help. For example, if your child is struggling to finish a task, offer some encouragement or assistance.

- Structure and routines should be provided. A regular schedule can help your child feel more in control and less overwhelmed. Try to stick to a regular schedule as much as possible. This will give your child a sense of security and prepare them for what is to come.

- Encourage self-talk that is positive. Encourage your child to use positive self-talk when he or she is feeling overwhelmed or angry. This includes telling themselves things like, "I've got this," or "I'm feeling calm." Positive reinforcement like this can help your child feel more in control of their emotions.

- Praise your child when they display positive behavior. It is important to praise your child when they are able to regulate their emotions successfully. This will help them feel good about themselves and encourage them to continue using their learned coping skills.

Tips for Parents of Children with ADHD on Developing Emotional Intelligence

There are several tips that parents of children with ADHD can use to help their child develop emotional intelligence. Below are some of the most effective tips for parents of children with ADHD:

- Model the desired behavior. As mentioned, modeling is a great way to teach children with ADHD emotional intelligence. Parents can model the desired behavior and provide positive reinforcement when their child exhibits it.

- Encourage self-reflection. Teaching children with ADHD to be self-aware can help them to better understand and manage their emotions. Parents can encourage self-reflection by asking open-ended questions and providing a safe and supportive environment in which their child can express their emotions.

- Set clear expectations. Parents should set clear expectations for their children and provide consistent and positive feedback when they meet those expectations. This can help to build self-confidence and encourage the desired behavior.

- Encourage practice. As with any skill, practice makes perfect! Parents should encourage their children to practice the skills they are learning to become more confident and comfortable using them.

- Be patient and understanding. Parenting a child with ADHD can be challenging, and parents need to remain patient and understanding. It is also important to recognize and celebrate small successes and progress, no matter how small.

How to Teach Children with ADHD Anger Management

Children with ADHD are often frustrated and angry and have a tendency to act out. However, the anger these kids feel is different from most other children their age. There are many ways that parents can help their children deal with anger, sadness, or frustration more healthily.

Anger is a normal emotion caused by our body's overreaction to something it perceives as threatening or harmful. We have all experienced anger at some point in our lives; it occurs when we are under too much stress and feel threatened by something. Children with ADHD can become frustrated, angry, and upset in a variety of ways. Everything becomes too much for them at times, and they are unable to cope.

ADHD is a disorder characterized by hyperactivity, impulsiveness, and difficulty focusing. Children with these characteristics struggle with anger and sadness because they have difficulty controlling their emotions in the first place. They are frequently angry because they feel powerless, and they are sad because they do not always understand why things happen the way they do.

Parents must be able to teach their children to recognize anger as a normal emotion and to become more aware of the situations that cause them to become frustrated. The following are some strategies for helping children with ADHD manage their anger.

- Keep calm. Parents must set a good example of how to deal with anger. When your child sees you become angry, it not only makes them feel worse, but it also makes them more likely to react negatively when they become angry themselves.

- Ignore it. Don't take things personally and avoid reacting to your child's rage. If they are angry, don't fight or argue with them; instead, ignore it. If your child becomes enraged at you, try to teach them a lesson so that they will not become enraged in the future.

- Act diplomatically. If your child throws a temper tantrum, do not become defensive, yell back at them, or use foul language. Try to keep your anger under control as much as possible.

- Seek assistance. Seek advice from a friend or a professional who has worked with ADHD children. Professional counselors are trained to deal with issues like these. They will be able to assist you in teaching your child that anger is not a way of life, but rather something that can be controlled through discipline and proper teaching methods.

- Encourage good behavior. These problems should not only be discussed at home but also at school. If your child has a temper tantrum at school, talk to the principal and ask that they be sure to keep it private. Explain that this is how they get angry and should not be encouraged.

Last but not least, you should find a doctor who can provide you with help if necessary. The doctor will want to make sure you are receiving proper treatment for your child's condition so that they can prevent these issues from becoming more severe or even going away completely.

Chapter 11: The Role of Self-Advocacy in Managing ADHD and Achieving Success in School and Work

Strategies for Assisting Your Child's Academic Success

As the parent of a child with ADHD, there are many things you can do to help your child succeed at school. To begin with, it is critical to get involved in your child's school life. Communicate with their teacher and stay current on the curriculum so that you can help your children review concepts they are struggling with or give them extra practice. Creating a routine and organizing study materials can also help children with ADHD focus on tasks and learn more effectively.

Furthermore, activities outside the classroom, such as tutoring or extracurricular activities, may benefit children with ADHD. Tutoring can provide children with personalized instruction that assists them in understanding difficult concepts while also providing positive reinforcement when they complete tasks successfully. Extracurricular activities, such as sports or clubs, allow children to explore new interests while also providing structure and organization after school.

Several factors will be considered when preparing for school success. As a parent, your priority should always be to ensure that your child is physically and mentally prepared to attend school. If you haven't already, schedule a physical with your doctor before the start of the school year.

Furthermore, you should discuss with your child some of the most significant challenges that they are likely to face at school and work with them ahead of time on strategies for dealing with some of these difficulties. Some of the signs or symptoms your child may experience at school may be better controlled with a little planning.

The following are the most common issues for which you should prepare your child:

1. Seating arrangements. Your child may have more or less difficulty paying attention and staying engaged in classwork depending on where they sit in class.

2. Social pressure

3. Modifying class schedules

4. Locker allocation and storage areas

5. Being the class's newcomer

6. Acquaintance with a new school calendar

7. Examining student files and paperwork (to avoid being overwhelmed)

8. Getting used to feeling like a prisoner in their own classroom (if they haven't already).

9. Having to make up classwork that they missed

10. Getting used to a new school schedule (changing recess periods, etc.)

11. Classroom discipline and how teachers treat students (Does it appear that teachers treat them differently than other students?)

12. Concerns about safety (Is there a lot of violence or bullying in the neighborhood? Are there any threats of violence directed at specific students?)

13. Children believe they are unable to discuss issues with adults while at school.

A child with ADHD may experience difficulties in school. These children are asked to perform the activities that they find most difficult during the day: standing still, silent listening, and focusing. The desire of the majority of these children to study and act like their unaffected classmates is perhaps the most vexing aspect. Children with ADHD are unable to learn in a traditional manner due to neurological deficiencies rather than a lack of motivation.

You can assist your kid in overcoming these deficiencies and the difficulties that school presents. You may talk to instructors about how your kid learns best and help your kid practice useful learning techniques both inside and outside the classroom. When used consistently, the following tactics may help your kid enjoy learning, overcome academic problems, and succeed in school and beyond.

Instilling Productivity and Motivation

Problems with organization and productivity can make it more difficult for a child with ADHD to stay motivated and do well in school and with friendships. In this chapter, you will learn how to support your child in becoming more motivated and better organized when performing tasks.

Your child with ADHD is likely to have difficulties doing what they're told, but that doesn't mean that they can't learn to follow instructions and be productive.

Here's how to help your child get things done:

- Be a positive role model for your child. If your child sees you doing it, they will find it easier to focus and complete chores. If you want your ADHD child to become more organized, the entire family should follow a set, consistent, and predictable schedule. That way, your child will see you doing similar things daily and will want to emulate you. Here are some tips for successfully modeling productivity to your child:

- Problems should be actively resolved. When it comes to resolving children's fights and overcoming boundary testing, all parents face a daunting task. When a child is struggling even more, the best way to teach them is to demonstrate how to avoid problems, listen to and communicate feelings, and compromise.

- Involve them in decision-making. All families benefit from sitting down and discussing problems with their children, regardless of their age or health. Some families meet weekly, while others prefer to sit down at dinner to discuss current plans and goals.

- Keeping up with the schedule. A family calendar with everyone's schedules and chores displayed shows how hard everyone is working and helps to avoid scheduling conflicts.

- Emphasizing rules and routines. Having simple, consistent, and visible routines throughout the day helps your child keep track of what to do.

Career and Life Planning

Adolescence is a time of opportunity and change. It can be hard to know what's best for your child, especially if he or she has ADHD. Learning about their diagnosis and what to expect can take time, so you must find out as much as possible before making any decisions that could affect your child's future.

Here are some things to think about:

- Lots of people with ADHD have great careers and wonderful lives. Your child may need extra support, but it's likely that he or she can still have a good education, a successful career, and an active social life. It's important to find out more about ADHD. The diagnosis will explain why your child is behaving the way they are at school or home. Knowing that there's a reason for this behavior can be very important for you and your child.

- Adolescence is a time of change. As your child gets older, you'll need to think about developing their social and academic skills in new ways, but it's also an exciting time of getting started in a job and finding out who they are.

- Ask yourself what you'd like for your child to do over the next ten years of his or her life. It's important to have realistic long-term plans, but it's also important to remember that time passes quickly.

- It's worth thinking about the positive things you can do now while they're still young. They've only got a few years left at school, so it's easier to make changes than later on. You can give those lots of opportunities for new things, even if they don't seem particularly popular at the moment.

- It's a good idea to make sure that your child has some structure at home. They're likely to have very different interests as they get older, so it's helpful if tasks are organized and simple.

- You can't do everything for your child, but it's likely you'll find things you can do that give you both more control over the situation. You don't want to teach them about making choices, but it's worth giving them the skills to recognize opportunities for change.

- It's a good idea to talk about your expectations for your child, as well as their friends and family. You don't want to hold back on saying what you'd like them to achieve, but you don't want them to feel pressured into doing something that's not right for them.

- Also, talk about life goals and planning for the future at different stages of your child's life. When it comes to choosing their future, it's easier if they have time to reflect and make decisions about their own needs, rather than just accepting what you say. As their skills change, so does what they're interested in learning or doing as well as how to do it. It's important to encourage them to learn new skills, but you're more likely to feel positive if they can still do what they want as they get older.

- It's worth thinking about your child's different interests and abilities. Some children become quite focused on very particular subjects. This can be helpful for certain careers, but it's also important that they have a wide range of interests and are able to take on challenges as well.

Chapter 12: The Available Treatment Options for ADHD, Including Medications and Behavioral Interventions

Treatments and Medications

Finding the best treatment for your ADHD child can be difficult. There are numerous options available, and it can be difficult to determine which is best for your child. This chapter will provide an overview of some of the most commonly used treatments and medications for ADHD in children. We'll also give you some pointers on how to pick the best option for your family.

Medication may be an effective treatment option if your child has been diagnosed with ADHD. ADHD medications are classified into two types: stimulants and non-stimulants. Discuss with your child's doctor which type of medication is best for them, and keep track of their symptoms so you can see how well the medication is working.

Stimulant Medication

Stimulants are the most commonly prescribed type of ADHD medication, and they work by increasing dopamine and norepinephrine levels in the brain. These medications aid in the enhancement of focus, concentration, and impulse control. In general, stimulant medication is very effective in treating ADHD symptoms.

However, there are potential side effects, as with any medication. Methylphenidate (Ritalin) and dextroamphetamine are two common stimulant medications used to treat ADHD (Adderall).

Stimulant medication is intended to help people with ADHD improve their focus, concentration, and impulse control. The majority of people who use stimulants report feeling calmer and better able to focus on tasks. Stimulant medication can help children with ADHD perform better in school and make friends more easily.

It is critical to remember that each child reacts differently to medication. You may need to try several different types or doses before determining which one works best for your child. Stimulant medications typically begin working within 30 minutes to an hour of administration. The effects usually last 3-6 hours before they wear off.

Stimulant medications are frequently prescribed to people with ADHD due to their effectiveness in alleviating symptoms. The stimulants in the medication work by increasing neurotransmitter levels in the brain. As a result, the brain receives a shot of norepinephrine and dopamine, which improves symptoms such as hyperactivity, impulsivity, and inattention in ADHD patients.

Although stimulants are frequently used to treat ADHD and are approved by the Food and Drug Administration (FDA) for use in children, many who use them do not respond to treatment or simply cannot tolerate it. There is also the case of people preferring one type of stimulant over another.

Here are some of the most common side effects you can expect when using stimulants: Irritability, dizziness, decreased appetite, increased anxiety, and insomnia are all symptoms. Tics, blurred vision, mild stomach aches, increased heart rate, blood pressure, and nausea are some of the less common side effects.

It is beneficial to be aware of and anticipate these side effects because they influence your willingness to take or adhere to the medication. Consult your doctor if your child experiences side effects from stimulant medications. Nothing should be left to chance. This is done so that you can safely stop taking the medication or adjust the dosage while under medical supervision.

Focalin (dexmethylphenidate), Adderall (amphetamine and dextro-amphetamine), Dyanavel XR (amphetamine), Vyvanse (lisdexam-fetamine), Daytrana or Concerta (methylphenidate), Zenzedi or Dexedrine (dextroamphetamine), Ritalin, Methylin, Metadate CD (methylphenidate), and Desoxyn (methamphetamine) are the most

commonly used.

Psychostimulants, or stimulant pharmaceuticals, are the most often recommended treatments for ADHD. The levels of neurochemicals known as neurotransmitters seem to be increased and balanced by stimulants. These drugs can work quickly and effectively to reduce the symptoms and indicators of hyperactivity and inattention.

Finding the proper dosage may take a while since it differs from kid to kid. Additionally, the dosage may need to be changed as your kid gets older or if serious adverse effects appear. Consult your doctor about any potential, stimulating side effects.

The most common side effects of stimulant medication are decreased appetite, trouble sleeping, anxiety, and irritability. These side effects are usually mild and go away after a few days or weeks as your body adjusts to the medication.

Non-Stimulant Medications

Non-stimulant medications work by increasing norepinephrine levels in the brain. Atomoxetine (Strattera) and guanfacine are two common non-stimulant medications used to treat ADHD (Intuniv).

There are a few things you can expect if your child begins non-stimulant medication for ADHD. To begin with, it may take several weeks for the medication to begin working. Don't be disheartened if you don't notice an immediate improvement. Second, non-stimulants typically have milder side effects than stimulants.

Although stimulants are often the first line of treatment for many people with ADHD, non-stimulant medication options are also available. The basic idea behind these medications is as follows:

- When stimulants have an excessive number of side effects

- For those who have a history of drug use

- When you are unable to respond to stimulants

- For people who have a history of certain heart conditions

- For those who have a history of bipolar disorder

You can give your child the following non-stimulant medications:

- Strattera. Strattera (Atomoxetine) was one of the first medications approved by the FDA for the treatment of attention deficit hyperactivity disorder in adults and children over the age of six. This medication may cause vomiting, fatigue, agitation, irritability, dry mouth, decreased appetite, stomachache, increased blood pressure, dizziness, nausea, and an increase in heart rate.

- TCAs are tricyclic antidepressants. Tricyclic antidepressants are not technically ADHD medications, but they are used for treatment off-label. Tofranil (imipramine), Norpramin (desipramine), Amitriptyline, and Pamelor are some of the most commonly used drugs in this category (nortriptyline). Side effects of these medications include vivid dreams, drowsiness, dry mouth, insomnia, constipation, headaches, stomachache, and blurred vision.

- Effexor (venlafaxine) is another antidepressant off-label ADHD medication. It aids in mood enhancement and concentration. Tremors, anxiety, nausea, sleep problems, dry mouth, and sexual problems are common side effects of the drug in adults.

- Wellbutrin (bupropion) is yet another type of antidepressant medication. It has been shown to reduce depression and ADHD symptoms in many users. However, some Wellbutrin side effects include insomnia, irritability, worsening of pre-existing tics, and weight loss due to decreased appetite.

- Anti-hypertensive medications. Other medications used to treat ADHD include blood pressure medications such as Tenex (guanfacine) and Catapres (clonidine). They help to manage ADHD symptoms, but they can cause fatigue, stomach pain, low blood pressure, nausea, dry mouth, insomnia, dizziness, and drowsiness.

Strattera is the most studied non-stimulant medication in this section for use as ADHD treatment in children and adults. As a result, studies show that it has fewer side effects than others, such as TCAs. Strattera is also more effective than Wellbutrin for ADHD.

The most common side effects of non-stimulant medication are dry mouth and trouble sleeping. Other possible side effects include dizziness, headaches, irritability, stomach aches, and loss of appetite.

Carefully Administer Medicines

Make sure your kid takes the recommended dosage of their medicine as directed. Stimulants and the potential for misuse and addiction may worry parents. When given as directed by the doctor, stimulant medicines are considered safe for children. To determine whether the medicine must be adjusted, your kid must visit the doctor often.

Contrarily, there is the worry that some may abuse or misuse stimulant medications recommended for children and teens with ADHD. To ensure that your kid receives the proper dosage of their drugs at the appropriate time and to maintain their medication regimen safe:

- Handle drugs with caution. Drugs for ADHD shouldn't be administered to kids and teenagers without sufficient adult supervision.

- Lock prescription drugs away in child-resistant containers at home. Additionally, keep medications out of children's reach. It is dangerous and may be deadly to use too much stimulant medication.

- Don't send your child's medicine supplies to school. You must personally deliver any medicine to the health visitor or nurse.

How to Choose the Best ADHD Treatment for Your Child

Have you ever read about the potential side effects of ADHD meds and been worried? Some worry just like you. Even though physicians often advise parents to give their children prescription medications for ADHD, many parents are hesitant to do so. This is not to imply that medication is not used in the treatment of ADHD. The best course of action is to thoroughly consider your alternatives.

Stimulants are the most popular kind of drug used to treat ADHD. Ritalin, Adderall, Dexedrine, and Concerta are a few examples of well-known stimulants. These stimulants' adverse effects include, among others, sleeplessness, reduced appetite, mood fluctuations, headaches, sadness, and anxiety.

Tricyclics and clonidine are a few more ADHD medicines. Although the FDA has yet to approve clonidine for the treatment of ADHD, it has been authorized as a medication for high blood pressure. While clonidine is effective in reducing hyperactive symptoms, it does not affect other ADHD symptoms such as impulsivity and attention deficit disorder. It is often recommended with Ritalin, however, the two medications used together have been connected to four fatalities.

Tricyclics are useful for ADHD patients who are also sad or anxious, although they fall short of stimulants in terms of effectiveness. Tricyclics may cause a variety of side effects, such as dry mouth, dry nose, sleepiness, anxiety, weight gain, nausea, and vomiting. As you can see, every prescription drug for ADHD has some potentially serious adverse effects.

If you are concerned about the side effects of ADHD meds, try all alternative forms of therapy first before turning to medication. No matter how hard your doctor tries to persuade you, resist the urge to give your kid prescription medication. With a change in lifestyle and the use of homeopathic medicines, many parents and kids have had success.

Contrary to prescribed ADHD medication, a homeopathic cure is completely harmless. To restore equilibrium at the cellular level and treat the symptoms of ADHD, homeopathy combines the natural healing abilities of the human body with those of plants. Homoeopathy has highly promising success rates when used in conjunction with food restriction, behavioral treatment, and a healthy lifestyle. Long-term use of homeopathic medications is possible without fear of negative side effects.

There you have it, then. In extreme situations, medications for ADHD are useful, but because of their possible negative effects, they should only be used as a last choice. Although the results of natural therapy may be delayed, they will aid in your child's long-term rehabilitation, and best of all, they have no adverse effects.

Behavioral Interventions

Parental Therapy

You, the parent, will benefit from this therapy. This type of treatment should be used in conjunction with your child's behavior therapy. Consider parental therapy to be a type of parent education course. Every parent has wished, at some point that their child came with a parenting manual. Treatment for parents is going to be that handbook. It will show you how to deal with your child's various behaviors. This is your opportunity to discuss how their actions affect you. You will discuss how you handle his/her behaviors, such as yelling excessively or failing to be consistent with your expectations and consequences. The therapist will teach you how to deal with explosive disorder behaviors. Remember that your responses are very important to your child. They influence how they feel because your reactions, especially if negative, may indicate that you dislike them.

Parental therapy will provide you with the tools you need to manage your child's behavior at home. Teaching you how to improve your parenting skills can be intimidating and even insulting. However, you must keep an open mind because you cannot expect positive changes in your child unless you change for the better yourself. When you have the strategies and tools you need to deal with explosive behav- iors positively, you will begin to see changes in your child. They will notice when you stop yelling at them for not listening and instead gently remind them. These kinds of changes have a big impact on an explosive child's feelings.

Family Therapy

It is a therapy that is for the family. ADHD does not affect only the child; it affects the whole family. It is a disorder that is often disrup- tive to the family unit. The goal of family therapy is to help each member of your family cope with ADHD behaviors. The behaviors of your child affect each person differently. Family therapy will address each member of the family in private and as a group. It will teach each family member how to deal with their feelings about ADHD and how it has personally affected them.

That is an emotional form of talking therapy. Each session will give the entire family a chance to voice their feelings and concerns. Everyone is not expected to agree and everyone is not expected always to react the right way to ADHD behaviors. Family therapy can be quite emotionally-charged. Each person's feelings are valid, even negative emotions. Each session allows the family to talk to a neutral third party. The therapist will listen to each concern and will help the family communicate with each other in constructive, positive ways.

Cognitive and Behavioral Therapies for Children with ADHD

Cognitive behavioral therapy is one type of therapy that can help children with ADHD. Behavioral and cognitive therapies are types of therapy that help children develop skills for managing their symptoms.

A psychologist, psychiatrist, social worker, or another mental health specialist can provide social skills instruction, behavior therapy, parenting classes, and psychotherapy to ADHD children. In addition to ADHD, some children may experience sadness or anxiety. Counseling could help both the concurrent issue and ADHD in these situations.

These therapies can be delivered in individual or group settings by a therapist, psychologist, or another mental health professional. Among the most common types of behavioral and cognitive therapies used to treat ADHD are:

Talk Therapy

Another helpful therapy that can be helpful for children with ADHD is talk therapy. Talk therapy allows children to express their feelings and thoughts in a safe environment. It can assist children in processing their emotions and developing coping mechanisms for stress. Individual or group sessions of talk therapy are available.

Parent-Child Interaction Therapy (PCIT)

PCIT is a type of BPT that helps parents learn ways to build a more positive connection with their children. The program coaches parents on how to use praise and effective consequences to help shape their child's behavior. PCIT is typically recommended for children up to age 7 who have more positive interactions with their parents.

During PCIT sessions, the parent and therapist role-play different scenarios. The therapist then provides feedback on the parent's performance. After several sessions, the parent is then able to practice these skills with their child at home.

Parent Management Training (PMT)

PMT is a type of BPT that teaches parents how to manage their child's behavior. This type of program is typically recommended for parents with children under the age of 12 who have more positive interactions with their children.

During PMT sessions, the parent and therapist act out various scenarios. The therapist then evaluates the parent's performance. Following a series of sessions, the parent is able to practice these skills with their child at home.

Positive Parenting Initiative (Triple P)

Triple P is a more general BPT program that can be used with people of any age. It can, however, be tailored to address more severe behavioral issues. Triple P focuses on assisting parents in developing positive relationships with their children while also teaching them how to effectively manage difficult behavior.

Chapter 13: Famous Men with ADHD

Many people were diagnosed with Attention Deficit Hyperactivity Disorder as children. Despite this, they went on to make a name for themselves and leave their imprint on the world. There are many famous names on the list, some of whom have accomplished incredible things.

Albert Einstein

Spending weeks in his study working on the theory of relativity was an achievable lifestyle for this scientist, but remembering where he put his keys was not. While hyperfocus and intellectual resilience were among Einstein's many talents, he struggled with remembering everyday information and minor details, which made him appear eccentric and out of place.

TY Pennington

The former host of the television show Extreme Makeover: Home Edition is another well-known personality who was diagnosed with ADHD when he was younger. Pennington was diagnosed with the disorder when he was in his twenties. He was able to turn his high-energy personality and love of carpentry into a successful television career. He is also a published author, having written several books. Pennington is an example of someone who uses ADHD to his advantage rather than against him. What was perceived as hyperactivity as a teen was later regarded as high energy and passion.

John F Kennedy

The stern posture of the well-renowned president was unlikely to reveal that J.F.K. struggled with ADHD, but he's a living example of how one can master self-discipline and control!

Walt Disney

Building an empire that the entire world adores a half-century after his death necessitated ingenuity and the kind of joyful creativity that lives on in Disney projects to this day. Disney did not let ADHD hold him back, instead channeling his creativity into creating beloved characters such as Mickey Mouse, Donald Duck, Snow White, and other cartoons.

Bill Gates

Whether you like Gates or not, you have to admit that very few individuals in the world can match His success! Who could tell that his inspired work and quirky temper had to do with ADHD?

Conclusion

Thank you for taking the time to read this book. ADHD is not a curse, and it does not predict your child's future. There are numerous factors that could lead to this diagnosis, but it is not the end of the world; the fact that someone is slightly different from everyone else is not a flaw, and it may even be an advantage in some cases if the energy is channeled correctly.

The sooner you address your child's issues, the more likely you will be able to prevent academic and social failure, as well as related issues such as low self-esteem and underachievement, which can lead to delinquency or drug and alcohol abuse. Even though raising a child can be challenging at times, you can help increase your child's chances of success by creating supportive environments at home and school. Parenting an ADHD child can be a difficult and stressful experience. Knowing what to expect, which strategies may help your child's behavior, and utilizing treatment options are all important aspects of ADHD parenting.

Parenting a child with ADHD can be a difficult experience for families, but it doesn't have to be. Although learning how to successfully parent a child with ADHD takes time, it is possible. Children who receive positive parental attention and participate in activities with their parents are less likely to develop psychological or behavioral problems, including ADHD, according to research.

Your child will become more sociable, successful, and confident if you use the information in this book. Please feel free to highlight any important points in this book. Then, go back and reread what stood out to you, making notes or setting reminders to help you consistently apply the solutions shared in this book.

Do not be disheartened or discouraged if some solutions do not produce the desired results quickly. If you have a strong will and are determined to help your child shine in ways you know they can, this book will undoubtedly help you.

Creating strategies for children with ADHD entails creating a consistent daily schedule that includes activities that help them feel successful and calm. Children with ADHD require additional structure and rules because they may perceive life to be chaotic and unpredictable. Consistency, stability, and high behavioral standards help children with ADHD respond more positively to their emotions.

Parents can work on strategies for managing their child's ADHD by seeking support from other parents in similar situations and inquiring about ADHD treatment options with their pediatrician. By understanding the disorder and developing effective strategies, you can make the best of your family situation and help your child succeed.

If your child does not respond positively to your encouragement or has a problem with you, do not abandon them. They may require additional assistance from a third party to help them improve at home. Meet with a teacher or counselor who can assist your child with his difficulties and establish some behaviors that will lead to academic success.

As a parent of a child with ADHD, you have many options for assisting your child's success. It is not up to one or two methods, but it may take some time to discover what works best for your child. When it comes to having a child with ADHD, you should be prepared for anything because their symptoms can change quickly and unexpectedly. When raising children, it is critical to keep them engaged in activities and to encourage them in what they do so that they are happy and can maintain a positive self-image along the way.

It will also be necessary for you, as the parent of a child with this disorder, to take time for yourself, rest, and enjoy the company of other adults to take your mind off ADHD for a while. Couples must support each other by sharing responsibilities so that their partner can take a break now and then. If you are a single parent, you will need the help of family and friends to take breaks when necessary. Do not underestimate the importance of staying healthy to care for your child. Eat well and get as much rest as possible.

Your child, like any other child, has the potential to achieve great things or live a normal life, and you should accompany them on that journey, reminding them along the way of your unconditional love for them.

Children with ADHD will undoubtedly improve as they grow older and learn to control their impulsivity, but this will only occur if they are subjected to the proper supervision of good parenting and effective therapy. So, use the information in this book to help your child succeed in life because they deserve the best.

All the best.

References

ADDitude Editors, & Dodson, W., MD. (2022, July 11). What Is ADHD? Attention Deficit Hyperactivity Disorder in Children and Adults. ADDitude. https://www.additudemag.com/what-is-adhd-symptoms-causes-treatments/

ADDitude Editors. (2021, April 22). 10 Ways We Would Fix the U.S. School System. ADDitude. https://www.additudemag.com/slide-shows/how-can-we-improve-education-for-students-with-adhd/

ADHD (for Parents) - Nemours KidsHealth. (2020). Lily. https://kidshealth.org/en/parents/adhd.html

ADHD and Behavior Problems - Child Mind Institute. (2022, July 13). Retrieved December 27, 2022, from Child Mind Institute web- site: https://childmind.org/article/adhd-behavior-problems/

ADHD and School (for Parents) - Nemours KidsHealth. (2020). Anton. https://kidshealth.org/en/parents/adhd-school.html

ADHD and school changes. (2022, April 19). Centers for Disease Control and Prevention. https://www.cdc.gov/ncbddd/adhd/features/adhd-and-school-changes.html#:%7E:text=ADHD%20and%20schools&text=This%20can%20mean%20special%20education,organizing%20work%2C%20and%20frequent%20communication.

ADHD Centre. (2018, March 6). 4 Major Challenges for Middle School Children with ADHD. Retrieved December 27, 2022, from The ADHD Centre website: https://www.adhdcentre.co.uk/4-major-challenges-middle-school-children-adhd/

ADHD in Children - HelpGuide.org. (2013). Retrieved December 27, 2022, from HelpGuide.org website: https://www.helpguide.org/articles/add-adhd/attention-deficit-disorder-adhd-in-children.htm

ADHD in Children and Adolescents. (2020). Alice. https://www.aafp. org/family-physician/patient-care/clinical-recommendations/all-clinical-recommendations/ADHD.html

ADHD in the Classroom | CDC. (2022, April 19). Centers for Disease Control and Prevention. https://www.cdc.gov/ncbddd/adhd/school-success.html

ADHD Parenting Tips - HelpGuide.org. (2013). Retrieved December 27, 2022, from HelpGuide.org website: https://www.helpguide. org/articles/add-adhd/when-your-child-has-attention-deficit-disorder-adhd.htm

ADHD Treatment Recommendations | CDC. (2020, February 3). Centers for Disease Control and Prevention. https://www.cdc.gov/ncbddd/adhd/guidelines.html

ADHD: How to Help Your Child Succeed at School. (2017, April 6). WebMD. https://www.webmd.com/add-adhd/childhood-adhd/adhd-how-to-help-your-child-succeed-at-school

Alley. (2006, October 6). How Boredom, Fatigue, and ADHD Hurt Our Kids' Attention Spans. Retrieved December 27, 2022, from Attitude website: https://www.additudemag.com/child-not-paying-attention-in-class-or-at-home/amp/

Alley. (2009, March 19). Will My Child Ever Have a Best Friend? Retrieved December 27, 2022, from Attitude website: https://www. additudemag.com/help-your-child-make-friends/amp/

Angel, T. (2021, October 13). Everything You Need to Know About ADHD. Healthline. https://www.healthline.com/health/adhd

Attention Deficit Hyperactivity Disorder (ADHD). (2008, September 18). WebMD. https://www.webmd.com/add-adhd/childhood-adhd/attention-deficit-hyperactivity-disorder-adhd

Attention-deficit/hyperactivity disorder (ADHD) in children - Symptoms and causes. (2019, June 25). Mayo Clinic. https://www.mayoclinic.org/diseases-conditions/adhd/symptoms-causes/syc-20350889

CHADD. (2020, October 22). Understanding ADHD. https://chadd.org/understanding-adhd/

English, A. M., Peirce, A., & Chua, J. P., MD Ph.D. (2021, July 13). *Ways to Help Children with ADHD in School*. EverydayHealth.Com. https://www.everydayhealth.com/adhd/adhd-in-school.aspx

Guidelines in Practice. (2021, January 15). *Updated guideline on ADHD defines the role of primary care*. https://www.guidelinesinpractice.co.uk/neurology-/updated-guideline-on-adhd-defines-the-role-of-primary-care/454257.article

Just a moment... (2020). Nion. https://www.psychiatry.org/pa-tients-families/adhd/what-is-adhd

M. (2022, March 24). *Treatment for Children with ADHD*. HelpGuide.Org. https://www.helpguide.org/articles/add-adhd/treatment-for-childhood-attention-deficit-disorder-adhd.htm

Managing attention deficit hyperactivity disorder (ADHD) in children and pre teens. (2021, July 2). Raising Children Network. https://raisingchildren.net.au/school-age/development/adhd/managing-adhd-5-11-years

Miller, C. (2022, March 22). *What's ADHD (and What's Not) in the Classroom*. Child Mind Institute. https://childmind.org/article/whats-adhd-and-whats-not-in-the-classroom/

Newmark, S., MD, & Panel, A. A. M. R. (2022, July 11). *The ADHD Diet Plan: Healthy Foods and Supplements for Kids & Adults*. ADDitude. https://www.additudemag.com/adhd-diet-for-kids-food-fix/

NHS website. (2022, January 12). *Attention deficit hyperactivity disorder (ADHD)*. Nhs.Uk. https://www.nhs.uk/conditions/attention-deficit-hyperactivity-disorder-adhd/

Team, T. U. (2022, May 4). What is ADHD? John. https://www.understood.org/en/articles/what-is-adhd

Treatment for Children with ADHD - HelpGuide.org. (2013). Retrieved December 27, 2022, from HelpGuide.org website: https://www.helpguide.org/articles/add-adhd/treatment-for-childhood-attention-deficit-disorder-adhd.htm

Understanding ADHD: Information for Parents. (2020). HealthyChildren.Org. https://www.healthychildren.org/English/health-issues/conditions/adhd/Pages/Understanding-ADHD.aspx

Working with Teachers to Help Your ADHD Child Be Comfortable at School | Study.com. (2020). Retrieved December 27, 2022, from study.com website: https://study.com/blog/working-with-teachers-to-help-your-adhd-child-be-comfortable-at-school.html

I want to say a big thank you for purchasing and reading my book.
If you found value in reading it, please consider sharing it with
friends or family and leaving a review online.
Your feedback and support are always appreciated and allow me to continue doing what I love.
If you have any specific suggestions on how I can improve the book, please feel free to write to me privately at: smartpressbook@gmail.com

Bonus

101 Tips to Empower Children with ADHD with Essential Life Skills.

We know that parenting a child with ADHD can be challenging, which is why we are pleased to offer readers of our book "101 Tips for Enhancing the Life Skills of Children with ADHD: "an exclusive bonus that will provide additional support and resources.

The PDF contains practical tips for managing behavior, developing routines, and improving communication with your child.

The PDF is easy to download and can be accessed directly from your smartphone or tablet using the QR code. It is a convenient and portable resource that can be used at home, on the go, or while traveling.

We hope this bonus will be a valuable addition to your parenting toolkit and provide you with additional support and guidance in dealing with the challenges of parenting a child with ADHD. We thank you for choosing our book and wish you and your child the best on your journey to success!

Printed in Great Britain
by Amazon